LEGENDS OF CHIMA™

CHARACTER ENCYCLOPEDIA

Written by
Beth Landis Hester
and Heather Seabrook

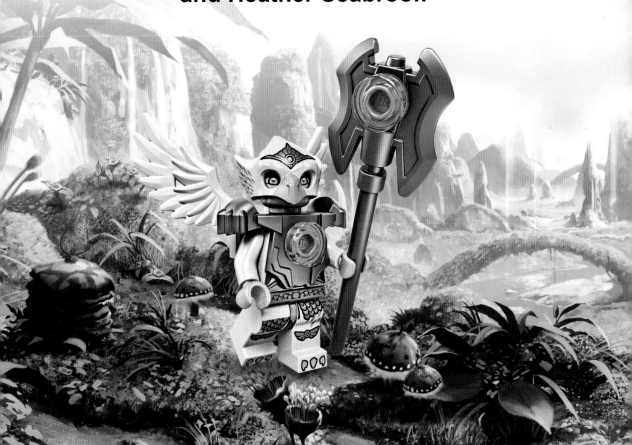

CONTENTS

WELCOME TO CHIMA

The mystical land of Chima is a lush paradise, full of tropical jungles, dark forests, sparkling rivers, and mysterious rocky terrains. Above it all, acting as a giant compass, hovers the magical Mount Cavora. Tribes of animals with unusual powers live here, ranging from brave and valiant Lions, to crafty Crocodiles. Recently, new tribes have emerged—including vain Spiders, snarling Saber-tooth Tigers, and, at the very top of Mount Cavora, the wise Phoenix. Come and meet them all!

ARE YOU READY TO MEET THE TRIBES?

HOW TO USE THIS BOOK

This book is a comprehensive guide to every LEGO® Legends of Chima™ minifigure released so far, accompanied by many of their vehicles, weapons, gadgets, and Speedorz™. The characters are all organized by tribe—for example, you can find King LaGravis (right) at the beginning of the Lion Tribe chapter. Data Files tell you all you need to know about a character's likes and dislikes, and gallery pages at the back of the book round up all the LEGO Legends of Chima sets and minifigures in their entirety.

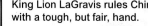
King Lion LaGravis rules Chima with a tough, but fair, hand.

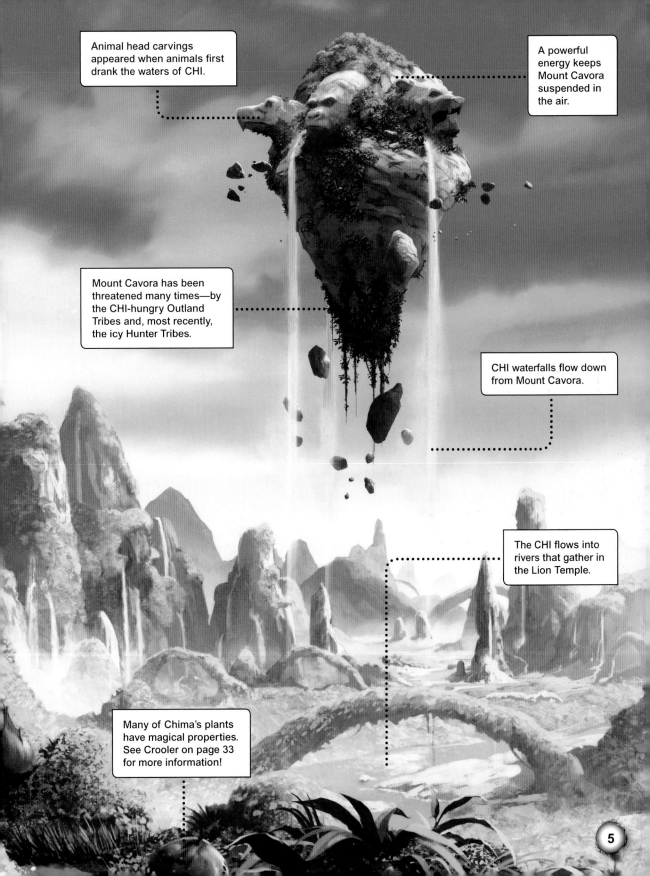

Animal head carvings appeared when animals first drank the waters of CHI.

A powerful energy keeps Mount Cavora suspended in the air.

Mount Cavora has been threatened many times—by the CHI-hungry Outland Tribes and, most recently, the icy Hunter Tribes.

CHI waterfalls flow down from Mount Cavora.

The CHI flows into rivers that gather in the Lion Temple.

Many of Chima's plants have magical properties. See Crooler on page 33 for more information!

HISTORY OF CHIMA

Chima was once a land of peace and harmony. All the tribes lived and worked together. Then a lightning strike revealed the powerful life force of CHI, flowing down from Mount Cavora. CHI gave any animals who drank from its waters extraordinary powers—such as the ability to walk on two legs, talk, and invent new machinery!

Sadly, fractions soon emerged. The powers of CHI were so awesome, that some tribes became greedy and sought more for themselves. The Lion Tribe established a system to distribute CHI fairly to all on CHI days. As new threats emerge to endanger Chima, can the tribes resolve their differences and join together so that peace can reign once more?

Cragger once sought CHI above all else, but he has since fought to protect Chima from evil.

Did you know?

There are three types of CHI: standard Blue CHI, Golden CHI won at Speedor races, and the rare Fire CHI.

Mount Cavora floats over the very center of Chima.

The Fangs and the Gorge of Eternal Depth

Tracks are perfect for Speedor races!

MAGICAL LAND
Many areas of Chima remain unexplored by its inhabitants. The Outlands, for example, is a dangerous territory, home to vicious and hostile tribes. It is rumored that this is where the mythical and powerful Legend Beasts (four-legged creatures that never drank from the waters of Mount Cavora) can be found.

SPEEDORZ™
The rocks used to carve the single wheel for these powerful vehicles fell from Mount Cavora. Speedorz™ are mostly used for racing monthly on CHI days—where the winner on the track is rewarded with Golden CHI—but are also handy for battles or traveling around Chima.

Speedorz are often customized with the colors of the tribe, or with extra accessories.

THE LION TRIBE

As Chima's greatest defenders, and the protectors of Mount Cavora's CHI Falls, the Lions live by a strict set of rules. Some think they are too strict—but the Lions know that without laws to govern the land, the mistakes of the past are bound to be repeated. The Lion Tribe values responsibility, bravery, and noble action. Above all, they stand for peace in Chima.

Prince Laval drives a speedy Lion Claw Bike.

PRINCE LAVAL
EAGER YOUNG WARRIOR

Brave, loyal, fun-loving, and heroic, Laval is the young prince of the proud Lion Tribe. He is eager to prove his worth as a leader, but anxious about the responsibility. Mischievous Laval would rather be playing jokes on his friends and seeking adventure at every turn.

SPEEDOR CHAMP
Laval loves riding his Speedor more than any other vehicle. He is king of the Market Day Speedor track!

Lion Tribe crown displays royal lineage.

 CHIMA FILE

LIKES Adventure, jokes, fun

DISLIKES Seriousness, water

BEST PALS Eris, Cragger

ARCHENEMIES Dark Tribes

Specially designed breastplate has a place just for CHI.

LION PRINCE
As prince of the Lions, Laval must keep peace among the tribes and help protect Chima's sacred CHI. Thankfully he has a great role model in his father LaGravis.

Did you know?
As a law-abiding Lion, Laval knows only too well that, under Chima's laws, it is illegal to use CHI before the Age of Becoming.

Lion Tribe crests on knee pads and belt.

CHI-POWERED LAVAL
ROARING CHAMPION

With CHI, Laval receives an extension of his raw animalistic powers. He reveals his powerful warrior spirit, making him a tough match for all his enemies—whether they are crafty Crocs or sneaky Scorpions.

Blue eyes reveal the presence of CHI.

SPECIAL EFFECTS
Like most of Chima's inhabitants, Laval uses CHI to give him extra strength in battle, and for powering weapons and vehicles.

Breastplate now shows a blue CHI symbol.

Massive paws are perfect for hand-to-hand fighting.

POWERING UP
Eager Laval had to learn patience when his Age of Becoming ceremony was interrupted by the Crocodiles. It was some time before he received his CHI and was able to power up for the first time!

Golden shield fends off other warriors.

SEE THE DIFFERENCE!
Compared to his regular form, CHI-powered Laval is more than twice as tall!

The Valious Sword is powered by CHI—only the most worthy and brave have the ability to use it.

Huge feet and strong legs make CHI-powered Laval a lightning-fast runner.

LAGRAVIS
KING OF THE LIONS

The stern-faced but soft at heart King LaGravis never loses sight of his enormous responsibilities. Most important of all is helping keep Chima in balance by making sure each tribe receives CHI—with a warning to "use it well, use it wisely."

Did you know?
LaGravis and Lavertus were inseparable childhood friends—until Lavertus was accused of stealing CHI and LaGravis was forced to exile him.

Honorous weapon

Golden crown bears symbols of CHI.

Determined expression shows fierce devotion.

BATTLE-READY
When battle is the only option, LaGravis leads by example. His swift Speedor is the fastest way to the front lines.

WISE RULER
LaGravis's gray beard and serious face are the result of many years of hard-won experience. He has seen what can happen when Chima is out of balance, and he's determined to protect it at all costs.

Brooch holds CHI and pins regal cloak to one side.

 CHIMA FILE

LIKES Peace among tribes

DISLIKES Seeing CHI used unwisely

BEST PAL Lavertus

ARCHENEMY Crominus

LEONIDAS
LOYAL FOOT SOLDIER

Fearless Leonidas never shrinks from battle—unless he becomes too confused to remember what to do! When Leonidas has more than one thing to think about, there's no telling what muddled mishap may follow.

Crooked smile shows that nothing gets Leonidas down!

🦁 CHIMA FILE

LIKES *Helping the Lion Tribe*

DISLIKES *Multitasking*

BEST PALS *Longtooth*

ARCHENEMIES *Any foe of the Lions*

Single strap holds CHI in place.

Simple, lightweight armor means Leonidas is ready for battle.

STANDING GUARD
Leonidas can usually be found guarding a post at the Lion Temple or in the company of his king, LaGravis. Although he can be forgetful, Leonidas has good intentions and always tries his best!

Did you know?
Leonidas is blessed with large vocal chords—his warning roar has woken the sleeping Lions and deterred intruders many a time.

LONGTOOTH
SEASONED VETERAN

Battle-scarred Longtooth has taken part in countless skirmishes during his many years as a soldier (as he will happily tell anyone who will listen). He still likes to be in the middle of the action, but unfortunately his best fighting years are behind him.

Long spear reaches enemies from the safety of the Speedor.

Helmet offers protection up top.

Pronounced fangs are true to Longtooth's name!

Triquill weapon

Deep scars to chest and face are souvenirs of past battles.

STILL SPEEDY
One place Longtooth is still as swift as he was in his youth? Racing along on his trusty Speedor, of course!

BATTLE-TESTED
Scarred by the fierce battles of his younger years, Longtooth looks like a force to be reckoned with. In reality, though, his worst enemies are his aches, pains, and a back that could go at any moment!

 CHIMA FILE

LIKES *The excitement of the front lines*

DISLIKES *Being too old*

BEST PAL *Lennox*

ARCHENEMIES *Anyone foolish enough to take him on in a fight*

Polished belt fixes CHI at waist height.

LENNOX
VEHICLES EXPERT

Laidback Lennox likes nothing better than riding fast and free on his Speedor or Lion Attack vehicle. In fact, anything on wheels is comfortable ground for this mechanical whiz—he knows just about all there is to know about vehicles of all shapes and sizes.

 CHIMA FILE

LIKES Speed, vehicles of all types

DISLIKES Staying in one place too long

BEST PAL Longtooth

ARCHENEMIES Crocs who think he's a brainless baby

Fangius weapon made from chimoralium material common in Chima.

READY TO GO
Lennox wears clothing similar to his fellow Lion guards, but subtle differences make his gear perfectly suited for traveling super-fast: an extra strap secures his CHI medallion in place, particularly handy for racing through the forest at top speed.

ARMED AND DANGEROUS
Enemies often underestimate Lennox, but the truth is this young Lion is both strong and skilled. He is a master of weapons and all types of vehicles—and is even unphased by driving the Lions' speedboats on water!

Did you know? The adventurous and easy-going Lennox is the youngest foot soldier of the Lion Tribe.

If Lennox took a leaf out of Longtooth's book, his belt could be just as shiny!

THE SACRED
LION TEMPLE
CHI SANCTUARY

At the foot of Mount Cavora, where the grasslands meet the jungle, sits the grand Lion Temple. Climb the magnificent stone steps, pass through the Lion-head gate with its terrifying open jaws, and you will find the home of the regal Lion Tribe and the Sacred Pool of CHI.

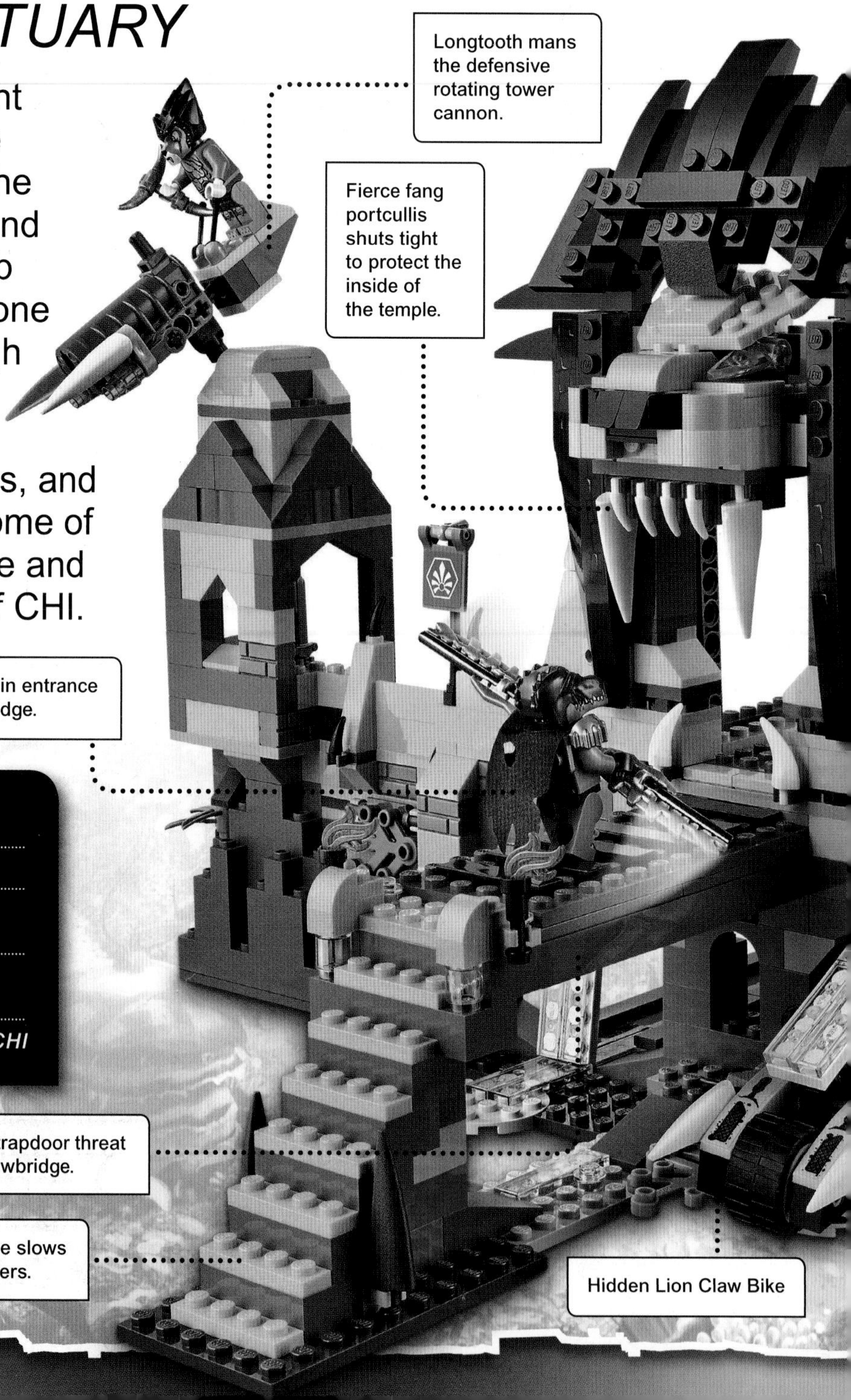

Longtooth mans the defensive rotating tower cannon.

Fierce fang portcullis shuts tight to protect the inside of the temple.

Cragger tries to gain entrance across the drawbridge.

⬡ CHIMA FILE

HOME TRIBE Lions

LOCATION Jungle/ grassland border

SECRET WEAPON Hidden trapdoor

PERFECT FOR Storing CHI

Concealed trapdoor threat beneath drawbridge.

Tall staircase slows down intruders.

Hidden Lion Claw Bike

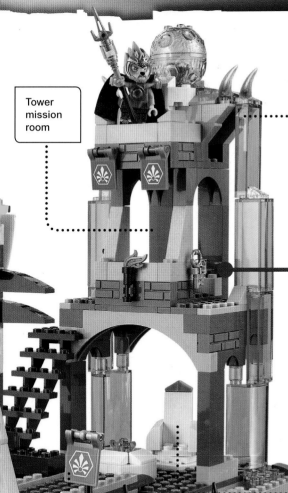

Tower mission room

CHI waterfalls

Golden key normally kept securely out of reach.

GO TO JAIL
The tower prison is a secure pen for captured enemies, caught trying to break into the Lion Temple. Longtooth turns the golden key to lock the door.

SACRED POOL
Chima's supply of CHI flows directly from the sacred waterfall and into the Lion Temple. To protect these all-important waters, the Lions have built gutters and channels to deliver every drop to the right location. The CHI then remains safely stored in its pool for handing out equally to all of the tribes.

Rotating king's throne

LAGRAVIS'S WATCHTOWER
King LaGravis guards the CHI orb and waterfall— situated at the very top of the Lion CHI temple and out of reach of enemy hands!

Crest symbolizes peace.

Jungle plants provide shelter and shade.

Launchpad for airborne vehicles.

LION
LEGEND BEAST

ANCIENT WARRIOR

An awesome figure in myth, the Lion Legend Beast is even more fearsome in the flesh. The hulking brute combines sheer feline force with mystic powers. Although a gentle giant when relaxing with his smaller Lion cousins, he can also leap fiercely to their defense when they're in need.

Majestic mane gives gravitas.

LAVAL AND THE LEGEND BEAST
Laval has a unique connection with all the Legend Beasts, but none more so than the Lion. Both are brave and noble, and each has faced his fear of water to save the other's life.

Stern warrior gaze masks a calm temperament.

Broad, strong paws are perfect for huge strides and leaps.

The Legend Beast allows Laval to ride on his back—a rare honor!

Tufted swishy tail can swipe enemies with force.

Did you know?
Like all Lions, the Legend Beast is terrified of water, but that didn't stop him from rescuing Laval from nearly drowning in a river.

RAW POWER

Having never drunk from the mystical CHI water to evolve human-like skills as the tribes did, the Legend Beasts have their own terrifying natural strength. This Lion doesn't need to walk on two legs to stalk and pounce on his enemy, or talk to get his message across.

Shoulder armor bears the symbol of the Lion Tribe.

Huge mouth can make a huge battle roar!

🦁 CHIMA FILE

LIKES *The Lion Tribe*

DISLIKES *Water*

BEST PAL *Laval*

ARCHENEMIES *Bats, Scorpions, Spiders*

Walking on four legs is a relic of ancient days.

LAVERTUS
AKA SHADOWIND

For many years, the banished Lavertus has lived on his own in the Outlands as a lone Lion among strange Outlands tribes and Legend Beasts. To most, the reason for his exile from Chima is a mystery—as is whether he will ever be able to return.

Pawprint mark is a symbol of uniqueness.

Stern expression warns that Lavertus is one tough customer!

SHADOWIND
In order to win CHI that will protect him in the Outlands, the exiled Lavertus disguises himself as the skilled racer ShadoWind. He then enters Speedor races to take the grand prize: Golden CHI!

MYSTERIOUS AND REMOTE
After many years fending for himself in the Outlands, Lavertus has developed strange habits and odd manners. He's not all that easy to get along with, but he has hidden talents, such as the ability to build things, that make him a strong ally.

Sturdy, handmade armor

Lion garb is tattered after years in exile.

Did you know?
Lavertus and Crominus once shared a love interest, Crunket, Queen of the Crocodile Tribe. The jealous Croc made sure his rival was out of the picture by orchestrating his exile.

🔶 CHIMA FILE

LIKES *Solitude, cupcakes*

DISLIKES *Trespassers*

BEST PAL *LaGravis*

ARCHENEMY *Crominus*

LAVERTUS'S
TWIN BLADE
AKA THE WINDSHADOW

Lavertus wasn't hemmed in by tradition when he built this one-of-a-kind flyer. His powerful helicopter uses technology scavenged from other Tribes to help it fly fast, fight tough, and arm its pilot for any battle that might come his way.

Rotor blades are angled and rotated to lift Lavertus away from Outland dangers.

HANDCRAFTED
True to Lavertus's unique nature, his Twin-Blade vehicle combines the silver color of Lavertus's handmade inventions with traditional golden Lion-like colors.

Long back stabilizes the Twin-Blade in flight.

Open cockpit is easy to hop in and out of.

Detachable maCHIguns are Lavertus's own invention.

Dual rotor blades give the handmade mech its name.

CHIMA FILE

HOME TRIBE Lions

CARRIES One Lion

SECRET WEAPON Detachable maCHIguns

PERFECT FOR Quick getaways

Ridged crank moves up and down to power the blades.

CHI-powered engine is under the hood.

Giant fang-teeth look Lion-tough.

LAVAL'S
ROYAL FIGHTER
WHEELS FIT FOR A PRINCE

When the battle lines are drawn and heavy-duty gear is needed, Laval hops into his Royal Fighter— a mean machine built for speed, toughness, and firepower! With a skilled driver in the armored cockpit, a gunner to aim the triple-barrel cannon, and four rubber tracks to race over any terrain, this fearsome fighter is hard to outmaneuver.

CHI-powered cannon spins for triple the firepower.

Lion mane acts as an adjustable shield.

OUTNUMBERED
With a gunner as well as a driver, the Royal Fighter easily outmans one lone Crocodile on foot. No sitting around on Laval's watch—everyone has a job to do in this well-equipped battle machine!

Fierce jaws open and close for gobbling up pesky Crocs!

Tough tracks can roll over any terrain.

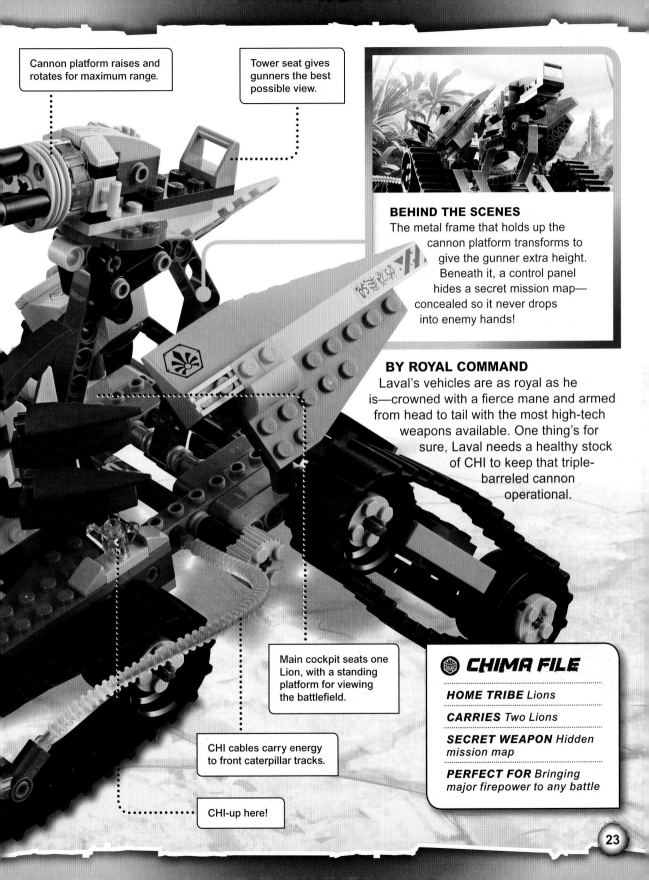

Cannon platform raises and rotates for maximum range.

Tower seat gives gunners the best possible view.

BEHIND THE SCENES

The metal frame that holds up the cannon platform transforms to give the gunner extra height. Beneath it, a control panel hides a secret mission map—concealed so it never drops into enemy hands!

BY ROYAL COMMAND

Laval's vehicles are as royal as he is—crowned with a fierce mane and armed from head to tail with the most high-tech weapons available. One thing's for sure, Laval needs a healthy stock of CHI to keep that triple-barreled cannon operational.

Main cockpit seats one Lion, with a standing platform for viewing the battlefield.

CHI cables carry energy to front caterpillar tracks.

CHI-up here!

CHIMA FILE

HOME TRIBE Lions

CARRIES Two Lions

SECRET WEAPON Hidden mission map

PERFECT FOR Bringing major firepower to any battle

LAVAL'S
FIRE LION
TOWERING TANK

Laval loves a good, fair fight, and this two-seater battle vehicle has everything he needs to strike fear into the hearts of even his newest enemies. The latest of his power vehicles has been adapted to include a convertible frame that will leave foes guessing, and swarms of missiles that will have them running for cover!

Flames trail behind in CHI power mode.

Lion-head design leaves no doubt who's in control.

FLASH CONVERTIBLE
This tough machine would frighten enemies just by standing still—but in motion it is amazing to see! As the tough track wheels roll over any terrain, a boost of CHI power can raise the machine's front and unleash the full fury of this claw-flexing, jaw-chomping vehicle.

Dual cockpit for Laval and one other

Launchers hurl missiles at enemies— up to four at a time!

Sharp claws strike enemies with piercing blows.

Thick treads suitable even for snowy and icy conditions.

Rear stability wheel keeps vehicle pushing forward even during transformations.

LENNOX'S LION ATTACK

BEST BUGGY IN TOWN

It's only natural that vehicles expert Lennox should have one of the fastest, sleekest machines in Chima! This versatile ride keeps the details simple: no bells and whistles, just speed and firepower!

ALL-TERRAIN FIGHTER

With Lennox on its back, the Lion Attack can race over any terrain, thanks to its wide-set wheels and flexible frame. But it's more than just a smooth ride—this mighty vehicle is a fighting machine!

Missiles aim in every direction with long-barreled launchers.

ROCK AND ROLL

Thanks to its wide wheelbase, tough tires, and expert driver, the Lion Attack can be seen racing through impossibly tough scrapes! With a bounce and a tip, Lennox is always steering into the action.

CHI Orb inserted in back as fuel

Wide-set frame keeps the vehicle from tipping on bumpy ground.

CHIMA FILE

HOME TRIBE Lions

CARRIES One Lion

SECRET WEAPON Rapid-fire disc shooter

PERFECT FOR Battling on any terrain

Claw fenders deter enemies from coming close.

Disc shooter is loaded and ready to shoot a rally of quick shots from gaping Lion's mouth.

Cables bring CHI firepower to front

LION TRIBE WEAPONS
ROYAL ARSENAL

The Lion Tribe relies on a powerful collection of weapons to protect sacred CHI before it is distributed, and to fight off those who would hurt their homeland. Wielding these weapons takes practice and an understanding of each one's special abilities, but if anyone can do it, the Lions can!

Valious sword was given to Laval by Lavertus for fighting in the Outlands.

CHI Banger weapons act like grenades.

Silver armor replaces Laval's old golden breastplate.

Long shaft of CHI runs through the center of the Valious.

LAVAL'S NEW GEAR
On his journey through the Outlands, Laval receives this shiny new gear and souped-up weapons from fellow Lion, Lavertus. He's never had such powerful weapons before, but he definitely needs them now to face the deadly Outland Tribes.

Extra-strong shield deflects blows from enemy weapons.

Did you know? As a young Lion, Laval learned to skillfully control weapons by fighting his target dummy: Sir Punch-a-lot!

ROYAL WEAPONS

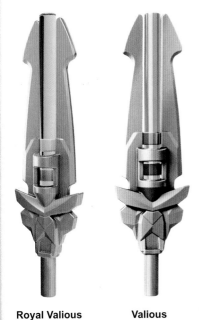

Royal Valious **Valious**

NOBLE SWORDS
Both these Valious swords were created to defend the Lion Temple and the Sacred Pool of CHI.

FANGS AND SPIKES

Royal Jabaka

Clubius Maximus **Hooxoar** **Fangius**

ATTACK GEAR
With long handles and tops designed to smash and whack, these are best for attacks.

LAVERTUS'S WEAPONS STASH

HOMEMADE CREATIONS
Banished from the rest of the Lion Tribe, Lavertus relies on his own handiwork to create and modify weapons that are truly one of a kind.

Dual Shadoglok

Duskoar

MODERN WEAPONS

Sonic Roarox

ZAPPER
Created with help from the Eagle Tribe, this high-tech weapon shoots a concentrated beam of CHI to stop enemies in their tracks.

THE CROCODILE TRIBE

The sneaky and slimy Crocodiles have always operated on the very boundaries of the laws of Chima. For the most part, they respect their fellow citizens, but they often take matters into their own hands. Even allies can't completely trust their underhand tactics. The Crocodiles don't see why they can't be in charge, so are constantly challenging the Lions' supremacy.

Prince Cragger powers a Croc mini boat through the swamp.

CRAGGER
CROCODILE PRINCE

Cragger has had an eventful life for one so young. Believing his parents to be dead, he has assumed the Crocodile throne and fought against other Tribes. Slowly, Cragger is learning to put aside his greed and ambition for the good of Chima.

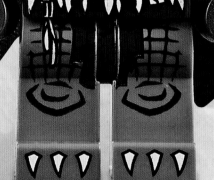

RIDE TO WIN
Cragger rides a specially designed Croc Speedor with a long, low body. An expert rider, Cragger's natural competitive streak emerges during tournaments.

FRIEND OR FOE?
Cragger has tried to befriend dangerous Wolves, foolish Rhinos, and untrustworthy Ravens in order to fight the Lions. Now he is learning that the best of friends, like Laval, are the ones that forgive you when you make mistakes.

Did you know?
Cragger's rivalry with his twin sister Crooler started early on in their lives—when she pushed his egg out of the family nest.

Left eye is missing and scarred.

 CHIMA FILE

LIKES *Winning*

DISLIKES *Being told what to do*

BEST PAL *Laval*

ARCHENEMY *Crooler, though he might not always know it*

Red cloak torn in battle

CHI-POWERED CRAGGER
WARRIOR WITHIN

Because of Cragger's often-malicious intent, his CHI power-up moment produces a red glow. Cragger first experienced CHI when an adolescent, and has hungered for its awesome power ever since—even at the cost of old friendships.

SEE THE DIFFERENCE
Cragger's inner warrior stands four times taller than his usual stature.

Triple-bladed Fangstaff

Massive snapping jaws

Sharp spikes running down spine

Tail acts as a vicious, swinging weapon.

Wide claws for powering through swampy territory.

GOOD INTENTIONS
A Leopard may not be able to change its spots, but Cragger is proving he can rethink his motivations. Soon this Croc may be wielding weapons glowing with positive Blue CHI energy.

31

CROMINUS
LONG-LOST KING

An uncompromising and protective leader, King Crominus doesn't always see eye-to-eye with the Lions. However, he still respects them. Crominus rules with common sense and fairness, and knows that fighting doesn't achieve anything.

Did you know?
Crominus's Royal Hakraxx weapon can only be used by the ruling King of the Croc Tribe. Its red crystal is one of only two in Chima.

ROYAL SPEEDOR
Crominus's Speedor is of traditional Croc Tribe design—long and low in the body with claw and fang decals.

Golden helmet crown signifies royalty.

BACK FROM THE BRINK
When King Crominus and Queen Crunket fell into the Gorge of Eternal Depth, everyone believed them to be dead. However, a gravity field broke their fall and they escaped into the Outlands—only to be captured by the tribes who live there!

Bone decorations

Regal cape

 CHIMA FILE

LIKES *His son, Cragger*

DISLIKES *The Gorge of Eternal Depth*

BEST PAL *Queen Crunket*

ARCHENEMIES *His captors in the Outlands*

CROOLER
MALICIOUS PRINCESS

Conflicted Crooler believes she is the rightful heir to the Croc throne, rather than her twin brother Cragger. She is scheming and cruel, pulling Cragger's strings like an evil puppet master, as only an older sister can—and also with the help of mysterious powers.

DESPERATE MEASURES
Chima is home to many magical plants and flowers. Crooler's persuader flower is powerful, but its magic is not unlimited, and it eventually runs out. Crooler must then find other ways to continue her ruthless plotting.

IN CONTROL
Crooler uses a persuader plant to manipulate others, including her brother. Playing on Cragger's insecurities and desires, she goads him into rushing headfirst into attacking the Lions in order to gain control of all the CHI.

Rebellious nose ring piercing

CHI fixed to homemade necklace decorated with teeth.

Did you know?
Crominus and Crunket warned Cragger not to trust his sister before they both fell into the Gorge of Eternal Depth, but to no avail.

Crooler relies on her ability to plan intricate plots, so scorns the use of weapons.

🐾 CHIMA FILE

LIKES *Manipulating others*

DISLIKES *Being caught out*

BEST PAL *Crooler relies solely on herself*

ARCHENEMIES *Everyone— Crooler trusts no one.*

Purple clothing marks Crooler as Croc royalty.

CRAWLEY
CHIEF CROCODILE THUG

A formidable foot soldier, Crawley is one of Cragger's best bodyguards. Small and nervous, but quick, Crawley is an obedient servant and would defend his master to the death. He can normally be found side by scaly side with fellow guard Crug.

Eager yellow eyes ready for battle.

Torn remnants of red clothing

Wily fighting frame

FAVORITE WEAPON
Crawley's Swampulsor is made from magnetic metal. The vicious red fangs are made from crook stone, a type of rock excavated from the swamps' depths. It even glows in the dark!

STING IN THE TAIL
Crawley uses his physical assets alongside fearsome weapons in battle. Opponents have frequently taken a heavy beating from his razor-sharp scales. While Crug is brutal and rough, Crawley is tirelessly unrelenting in a fight—together they make a formidable duo.

Did you know?
Crawley is secure in the knowledge that he is the top Croc soldier, whereas Crug is his second-in-commmand.

CRUG
BRUISING BODYGUARD

Cragger's hefty henchman, Crug, is big and strong but sadly dimwitted. Crug would follow any order of Cragger's, even if it was to jump into the Gorge of Eternal Depth. He is unquestionably willing to undertake any crazy task for his leader.

RECLESS MISSION
Crug would do anything for his beloved master Cragger, including stealing CHI from the Lions—a serious crime—on a simple Croc Swamp Jet, without any weapons.

🐾 CHIMA FILE

LIKES *Smashing, beating*

DISLIKES *Thinking too much*

BEST PALS *Cragger, Crawley*

ARCHENEMIES *Lions*

Did you know?
Despite his tough-guy image, Crug sleeps cuddled up with a stuffed toy frog called "Mr. FlipperLovey."

Metal replacement lower jaw

ARMED TO THE TEETH
Crug's jawline alone is a threatening sight, but even more so when combined with his favorite weapon—the Slugga—named after his favorite snack. The blacksmith of the Croc Tribe is an expert at making weapons from the metal and rocks found in and around the swamps.

Unusual dark brown scales camouflage with the dirtiest of all swamp mud!

THE CROCS' SWAMP HIDEOUT

HIDDEN LAIR

In the dank, dark Chima swamp lies this partly submerged hideout—home to a sneaky, slippery bunch of Crocs. Only the bravest dare venture into this dingy lair—passing through the snapping jaws entrance, and dodging missiles and foot soldiers. Enter at your peril!

PERFECT LOCATION
The hideout is built in the Crocodiles' natural habitat—the swamp. This is perfect for the reptilian Crocs, but less so for their furry enemies. Infiltrating this camp is a Lion's worst nightmare, as they must face their fear of water to reach it!

Leonidas escapes from the hanging cell while Crug is standing guard.

Huge snapping jaws can be triggered to slam down at any moment on unwelcome visitors.

Stolen Orb of Golden CHI

HIDDEN WEAPONS STASH
A hideout isn't complete without further hidey holes for storing extra weapons. Although, it looks like this stash is secret no longer, as Leonidas has stumbled upon it!

Burning torches light up dark swamp.

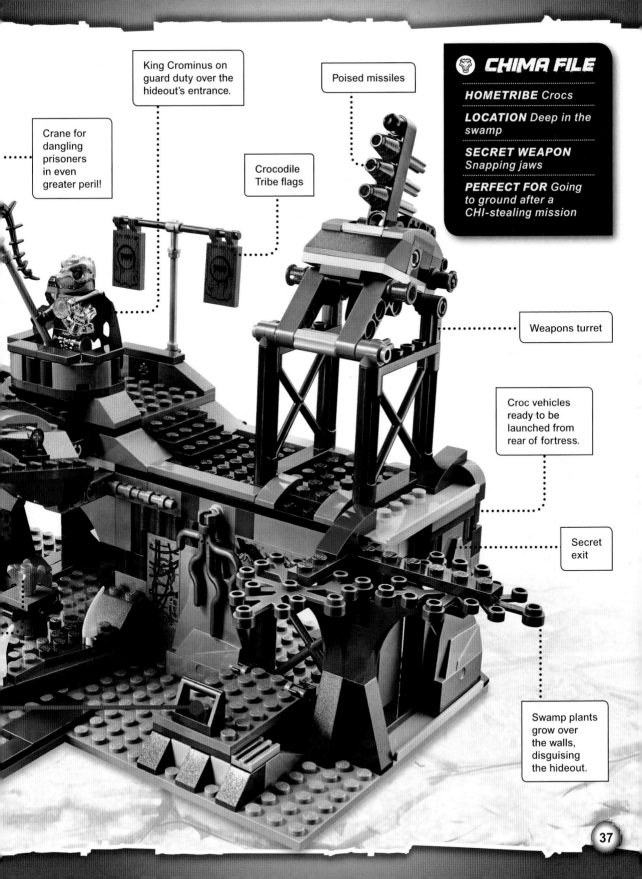

Crane for dangling prisoners in even greater peril!

King Crominus on guard duty over the hideout's entrance.

Crocodile Tribe flags

Poised missiles

CHIMA FILE

HOMETRIBE *Crocs*

LOCATION *Deep in the swamp*

SECRET WEAPON *Snapping jaws*

PERFECT FOR *Going to ground after a CHI-stealing mission*

Weapons turret

Croc vehicles ready to be launched from rear of fortress.

Secret exit

Swamp plants grow over the walls, disguising the hideout.

CRAGGER'S COMMAND SHIP
ROYAL CROCODILE CRAFT

This ferocious-looking ship with terrifying teeth and sharp decorative spikes is the Crocodiles' most intimidating way of traveling around their murky swampland. It powers through the sludgy water thanks to its brawny hind legs and propellers. Look out for its snapping jaws!

CRAFTY CROCS
Just like the Crocs themselves, their vehicle design is long and low—perfect for sneaking through the swamplands and lurking in damp, dark areas. Most of their vehicles can float in water, dive under the surface, and even move fast on land too!

Vicious articulated tail

Detachable boat

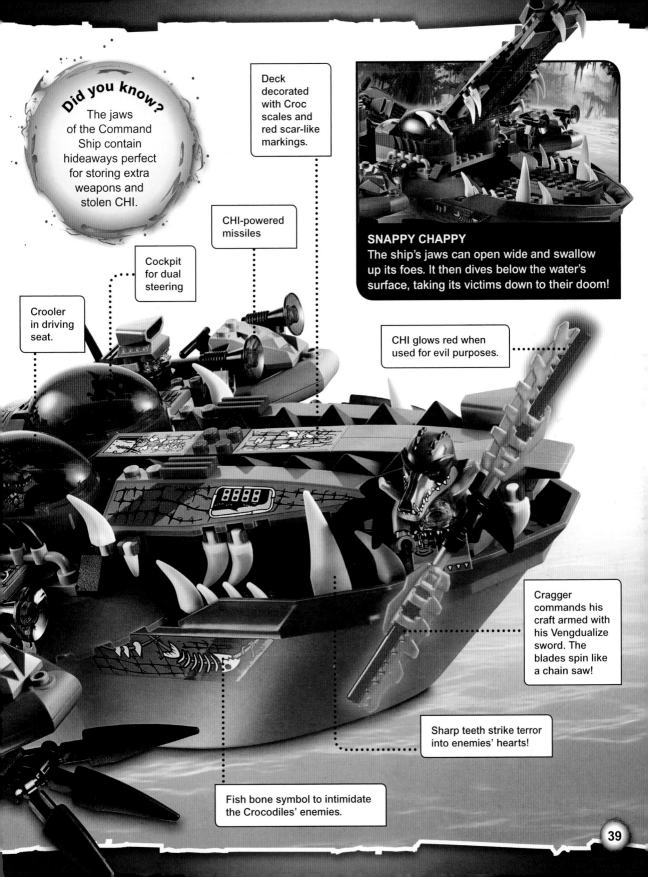

Deck decorated with Croc scales and red scar-like markings.

CHI-powered missiles

Cockpit for dual steering

Crooler in driving seat.

SNAPPY CHAPPY
The ship's jaws can open wide and swallow up its foes. It then dives below the water's surface, taking its victims down to their doom!

CHI glows red when used for evil purposes.

Cragger commands his craft armed with his Vengdualize sword. The blades spin like a chain saw!

Sharp teeth strike terror into enemies' hearts!

Fish bone symbol to intimidate the Crocodiles' enemies.

CRAWLEY'S CLAW RIPPER

ALL-TERRAIN VEHICLE

Crawley alone is terrifying, but the sight of him seated behind the ferocious snapping mouth of his Claw Ripper is even scarier. This vicious vehicle is specially designed to traverse the different areas of Chima, with powerful rear wheels and all-terrain treads.

SAFE DRIVING
The Claw Ripper has the ability to carry on driving even if the whole vehicle flips over! It is fitted with a safety cage to keep the driver in place—released by pulling a lever in the cockpit.

CHIMA FILE

HOME TRIBE *Crocodiles*

HOLDS *One Croc*

SECRET WEAPON *Snapping jaws can crush enemies*

PERFECT FOR *Making a quick escape*

Secret CHI chest concealed in rear.

Crawley sits securely in the one-Croc cockpit.

CHI GETAWAY CAR
Crawley has most fun when driving his Claw Ripper to raid other tribes' CHI stores. With a secret compartment to stash the booty until safely back at the Croc Swamp Hideout, once the CHI is in its confines it's as good as gone!

Caterpillar tracks can flip over for sideways driving.

Rotating tooth weapons

CROCODILE LEGEND BEAST

LIVING LEGEND

This oversized Crocodile's scales mask a heart of gold. The Crocodile Legend Beast is strong and tough, but also honorable, and proves time and time again to be invaluable assistance in times of need. It is not long before he has formed a firm friendship with Cragger.

SWIM STAR
Pursued by Bats, the situation for Chima's heroes looks hopeless—until the Crocodile Legend Beast leaps to the rescue, carrying Cragger to safety through the water.

SURVIVOR
Nobody believed that anything could survive in the Outlands. When the Crocodile Legend Beast returns to Chima accompanied by Queen Crunket, it demonstrates that the Outlands are survivable, if you know what to avoid!

Royal Vengious sword now glows blue

Cragger has a strong bond with his Legend Beast, particularly after it rescued his long-lost mother.

Tough scales are ideal for surviving in the inhospitable Outlands.

Powerful limbs are slow on land but fast in water.

CHIMA FILE

LIKES Swimming

DISLIKES Being captured

BEST PALS Any Crocodile

ARCHENEMIES Outland Tribes

41

CRAGGER'S FIRE STRIKER

FIERCE FIRE-BREATHER

When plains of ice advance across Chima, the Tribes must adapt to the new, tricky terrain. Cragger's Fire Striker combines snapping Crocodile features with red-hot Fire CHI technology. Hunter Tribes, beware this armored tank with scorching flames and fierce Croc teeth!

Bursts of flame provide extra speed

Cragger wearing armor gifted by the Fire Tribes

FIRE CHI POWER MODE!

What is the best defense against ice? Fire! Turbo-charged by mighty Fire CHI, the Fire Striker is packed with power. Two extending arms rise up to fire solid balls of flaming CHI. And just wait until the Hunter Tribes see the fire cannon hidden inside the snapping jaws of the vehicle's glowing mouth!

CHIMA FILE

HOME TRIBE Crocodiles

CARRIES One Croc

SECRET WEAPON Fire CHI ball blaster

PERFECT FOR Chasing the invading Hunter Tribes

Heavy-duty tires for executing sharp turns without skidding on icy ground.

Fire CHI locked securely in position

Did you know?
Fire CHI is so deadly to the Hunter Tribes that they cannot even touch it. This gives the Chima Tribes a fiery battle advantage.

HOT PURSUIT
When not in use, the Fire Striker's missile arms fold down for a more aerodynamic shape. Huge rubber tires with deep treads grip the slippery ice, so Cragger can zoom long distances without losing control.

Symbols of the Phoenix and the Fire Tribes

Fire ball shooters

Mouth breathes hurricanes of fire.

Snapping Crocodile jaws

Deadly fangs

CROCODILE TRIBE WEAPONS

SWAMPY CREATIONS

The Crocodile Tribe has some of the finest crafted weapons in all of Chima. An expert in his field, their blacksmith makes weapons from the rocks and metals found in and around the swamps. These dark metals have magnetic qualities useful in building and customizing weapons.

NEW GEAR

On their mission to find the Legend Beasts, Lavertus gives Cragger new armor and weapons. Cragger's CHI begins to glow blue instead of red—signifying that he now has good, rather than bad, intentions.

CHI-powered Scale Ripper for fighting Outland Tribes.

New, upgraded silver armor

Blaster fires pulse beams.

Sword blades extend from either side.

FIT FOR FOOT SOLDIERS

Krank

Jabaka Spear

Ripporous

Perfect for close, hand-to-hand combat, these basic weapons get the job done.

ANCIENT WEAPONS

Vengdualize

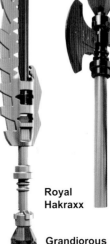

Vengious

Royal Hakraxx

Royal Sceptrok

Grandiorous

These weapons are symbols of power. The Vengdualize is handed down from royal father to son, the Grandiorous is the Crocs' oldest weapon and it shares a rare red CHI crystal with the Royal Hakraxx—which answers only to the King.

WEAPONS IN ACTION

CRUG'S SLUGGA
This simple blaster fires powerful pulse beams at Crug's opponents.

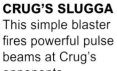

Slugga

CRAWLEY'S SWAMPULSOR
Designed for stealth operations, the Swampulsor has red glow-in-the-dark fangs made out of crook stone: a rock from the bottom of the swamps.

Swampulsor

CRAGGER'S VENGIOUS
The Golden Vengious is an upgraded version of the Vengious, which has since been handed over to the Wolves.

Golden Vengious

THE EAGLE TRIBE

From their wide reading, this scholarly tribe is well aware of Chima's history and the danger of unbalanced CHI. So while they'd rather be browsing the library with a book under each wing, the Eagles are always ready to defend their friends and take to the skies for the good of the land.

Eris wields the Eagles' most precious weapon—the Eglaxxor.

ERIS
STEADFAST FRIEND

Eris is proud of her home village, but this adventurous Eagle also loves to explore exciting new parts of Chima with her best friend Laval. Brainy Eris is always eager to learn new things and is happy to share her knowledge of the tribes and terrains of Chima.

Golden crown detailing on helmet

Lightweight armor is protective without slowing down flight.

Golden chainmail in soft feather pattern.

FEARLESS FLYER
Strong wings are the signature feature of every Eagle. But superior Eagle technology means that Eris can soar to great heights on her Speedor too! Eris feels right at home in the sky.

BEAUTY AND BRAINS
Eris's beauty has charmed many in Chima, but it is her amazing mind that really sets her apart. When adventures take her far afield, Eris has the knowledge to communicate well with different tribes and find her way back home again. Her jokes, however, aren't as funny as she thinks they are!

Did you know?
Rogon the Rhino is one of Eris's many admirers. Despite their many differences, Eris has a soft spot for him, too!

CHI-POWERED ERIS
SWIFT AND STRONG

With CHI to power her, Eris can fly at lightning-fast speeds to help her friends and can strike with amazing power to battle her enemies. Not a natural fighter, she doesn't often use CHI, but when she does it's something to behold!

SEE THE DIFFERENCE
CHI-powered Eris becomes twice as tall—but her wings expand even farther, stretching far above her head!

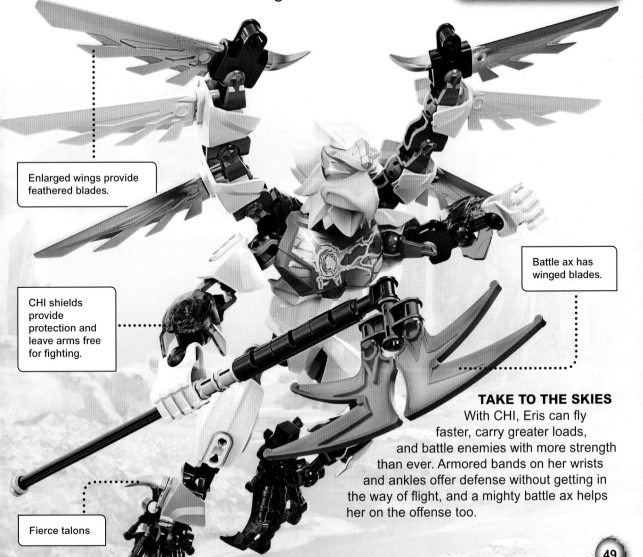

Enlarged wings provide feathered blades.

CHI shields provide protection and leave arms free for fighting.

Battle ax has winged blades.

TAKE TO THE SKIES
With CHI, Eris can fly faster, carry greater loads, and battle enemies with more strength than ever. Armored bands on her wrists and ankles offer defense without getting in the way of flight, and a mighty battle ax helps her on the offense too.

Fierce talons

EQUILA
DIVEBOMBING DAREDEVIL

🐾 CHIMA FILE

LIKES Target practice

DISLIKES Peace and quiet

BEST PAL Ewar

ARCHENEMIES Ravens

Guardsman Equila is known for his skill in flying and his amazing aim when targeting enemies from above. He's a fierce fighter who can always be found in the thick of the battle!

Steely gaze fastened on target.

Black-rimmed goggles help Equila to see clearly from great heights.

TRUSTED GUARDIAN
Equila has special responsibility for the Eagles' most precious weapon, the Eglaxxor. It's his job to make sure it stays safe and out of enemy hands.

READY TO FLY
As an Eagle guard, it is Equila's job to be strong, smart, and brave—and he excels at it. He is always ready for a high-flying adventure—so when the Eagles are under attack, he'll take to the skies with a flap of his powerful wings, take aim, and give his best shot for Chima!

Did you know?
On Market Days, Equila sometimes acts as the announcer for Speedor races. Ready, set, go!

EGLOR
MASTER OF PROJECTILES

With Eglor's precisely calculated launches, sticks and stones can hurt your bones—and your toughest tanks, too! Eglor can figure out the right angle and speed to make simple weapons cause major damage.
  If only the enemy would stay put until the calculations were complete...

Monocle brings targets into view and magnifies tiny scribbled calculations.

Unique dark feathers

Silver buckles for strapping Eglor into his newest contraption, or attaching handy gadgets.

BLUE BIRD
His dark blue feathers are unique in this tribe, but there are many qualities that Eglor shares with his fellow Eagles, such as intelligence, an analytical mind, and a willingness to fight for the good of Chima.

CHIMA FILE

LIKES Math and science

DISLIKES Being rushed

BEST PAL Whatever problem he's puzzling over now

ARCHENEMIES Ravens

UP, UP, AND AWAY!
It's not just missiles that Eglor can make soar: With a well-placed ramp and some clever calculations, Eglor can make his winged Speedor catch some air, too!

EWAR
DEDICATED SOLDIER

Give eager Ewar a good battle plan, and he'll practice it, learn it by heart, and put it into action with precision. As long as he has a clear mission in mind, Ewar is unstoppable! But if that plan goes awry, look out—this single-minded warrior will come to a screeching halt!

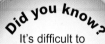

ON TRACK
Small and nimble, Ewar's Acro-Fighter glides in and out of tight spots on its adjustable double skis. With this vehicle, Ewar is always on the move.

Pure white brow gives Ewar a crisp, clean look.

STEELY FOCUS
With strength, determination, and a loyal heart, Ewar can do anything... except change course. He values thorough preparation and total dedication to the cause at hand. But being flexible? That's something for the other birds!

Did you know?
It's difficult to tell Ewar and Equila apart. Ewar's head has less feather patterning and he doesn't need those goofy black goggles.

Muscled torso is a sign of a highly trained warrior.

 **CHIMA FILE**

LIKES Well-laid plans

DISLIKES Spontaneity

BEST PAL Equila

ARCHENEMIES Ravens

Simple uniform is the perfect fit for Ewar's straightforward personality.

EWALD
TRIBAL LEADER

As a ruling elder on the Eagles' tribal council, Ewald has an important role to play in the leadership of Chima. Ewald will always do what he must to protect the Eagles and help maintain peace in Chima, but in truth he'd rather read books in Eagle Spire's library than talk battle plans and politics.

Golden headdress with Eagle symbol signifies Ewald's ruling status.

Long robes are suitable for a life of study and debate, rather than action.

Detailed gold embroidery is the work of the Eagles' finest tailors.

🦁 CHIMA FILE

LIKES *Scholarly discussions*

DISLIKES *Hasty decisions*

BEST PAL *The Eagles' library*

ARCHENEMIES *Ravens*

EDUCATED ELDER
Peaceful Ewald is a firm believer in the power of the mind. He spends his days in pursuit of knowledge, often with his beak in a book and his mind faraway from everyday cares. But don't let the scholarly robes fool you: He can also be a feisty fighter when duty calls!

Did you know?
When Wolves and Ravens attack Eagle Spire, Ewald helps fight them off by throwing his heaviest books at their heads!

THE EAGLE
CASTLE
FEATHERED FORTRESS

For protecting the Eagles' share of CHI, there is no safer place than this inaccessible clifftop castle. From its high vantage point, Ewald can keep a look-out from his lofty throne.

HIGH AND MIGHTY
The Eagles are often accused of having their heads in the clouds. With their tall and imposing clifftop home, it's easy to see why!

⬡ CHIMA FILE

HOME TRIBE Eagles

LOCATION
Remote mountain peak

SECRET WEAPON
Booby-trapped CHI towers

PERFECT FOR Storing CHI high out of reach

Ewald's golden throne sits on high, accessible only by flight.

Winged doors rise open to reveal Golden CHI.

WINGED WONDER
No ordinary building, the Eagle Castle stores a wealth of knowledge so the Eagles can continue their scholarly learning. This peace-loving tribe would always rather watch a battle from the safety of above than venture down and get involved!

Extra weapons

Lennox and Worriz battle for CHI from their Speedorz.

Column holding CHI levered to avoid capture.

EGLOR'S TWIN BIKE
DUAL-PURPOSED DRIVE

Blazingly fast to drive, the powerful Twin Bike carries Eglor over land at incredible speeds. When the enemy takes to the sky, a high-tech transformation will have this bike soaring high and continuing the chase through the air.

ROAD WARRIOR
Huge tires and tons of power make this machine a favorite of Eglor's, the weapons expert. With wings tucked in tight, it can tear over land in a flash, showering enemies with firepower from multiple missiles.

⊛ CHIMA FILE

HOME TRIBE Eagles

CARRIES One Eagle

SECRET WEAPON Transformative powers

PERFECT FOR Pursuing runaway Ravens

Wings adjust for the most aerodynamic design on the road or in flight.

Hidden vents help keep the engine running smoothly.

Oversized tires stand up to bumpy roads.

CHI slots into place in front of driver's seat.

Slim missiles offer firepower without causing drag.

AIR COVER
A few quick changes, and this king of the road becomes the king of the skies! Rotated tires become boosters, the driver's seat becomes a cockpit, and the wings open wide to carry Eglor through the air and in hot pursuit of CHI thieves.

EQUILA'S EAGLE
ULTRA STRIKER
BATTLE MACHINE

To be worthy of one of the Eagles' bravest warriors, a vehicle would have to be truly special. The Ultra Striker is the perfect match for Equila's daring and skill, combining speed, firepower, and high-tech surprises with every clever switch and transformation.

BATTLE PLAN

Winged, clawed, and heavily armored, this is one serious machine! As its giant treads roll over rough terrain, the Ultra Striker's adjustable armor offers major protection to the driver inside. That gives Equila plenty of time to raise and lower the missile-loaded wings and take aim at enemies from his raised cockpit... then fire the CHI-powered guns and storm past enemy lines!

Rear wheel beneath tail provides extra power and bursts of speed.

Powerful rocket shooter

Cables full of flowing CHI power

Gauge displays remaining CHI levels within Ultra Striker.

 CHIMA FILE

HOME TRIBE Eagles

CARRIES One Eagle

SECRET WEAPON
Ejectable escape pod

PERFECT FOR
Ploughing into battle

Did you know?
Like many of Chima's toughest vehicles, it takes two Orbs of CHI to power the Ultra Striker.

Wide wings angle and position missiles for perfect aim.

Equila in the shielded pilot's seat, safe from attack

ESCAPE POD
Should the worst happen, and the Ultra Striker can't escape from a tricky situation, its winged escape pod can be ejected, firing Equila to safety.

Wings attached to cockpit for flying to safety after pressing the eject button.

Ridged tracks roll over any terrain.

Sharp articulated claws keep enemies at bay.

ERIS'S EAGLE
INTERCEPTOR
PREDATOR IN THE SKIES

When Eris is at the controls of her Interceptor, she zips through the clouds, shooting down enemy jets, and showing Chima that the Eagles are no pushovers. With its turbo-powered jet engines, this tech-heavy plane is so fast, it's tough to spot—let alone catch!

Feather extensions adjust for optimal aerodynamics.

Eris's seat in the cockpit is ejectable in case of emergency.

Beak-shaped nose slices through the air.

CHI store located at rear

BIRD OF PREY
The Interceptor looks the part of a terrifying predator, and its battle capabilities are just as fearsome. Wing-mounted missiles, razor-sharp grasping claws, and convertible booster jets make it a nearly unbeatable opponent in battle. And with a pilot like Eris, there's little this plane can't do!

Moving claws grasp and grab to capture or attack.

Legs flip back to reveal jet boosters for a burst of speed.

CHI THIEVES
The Interceptor's CHI supply is stored in a rear hatch, which lifts up for easy access—unfortunately overly easy, as Razar has found the haul and is about to make off with it. Perhaps Eris needs some rear wing mirrors!

 CHIMA FILE

HOME TRIBE *Eagles*

CARRIES *One Eagle*

SECRET WEAPON
Supersonic speed

PERFECT FOR
Airborne battles

EAGLE
LEGEND BEAST
POWERFUL PROTECTOR

The Eagle Legend Beast shares many characteristics with her fellow Eagles, though not the ability to talk or build machinery. However, she has a primal, magical power that, with the other Legend Beasts, is Chima's salvation when the waterfalls of Mount Cavora run dry.

Strong back can support a rider—and her weapons.

Wide wings soar through the Outlands and over Chima.

TERRIFIC TEAM
The Legend Beast has all the physical strengths that the Eagles have built into their best machines—sharp talons, wide wings, and a fierce gaze. Together with the Eagles' highly developed minds, they make quite a team!

ERIS AND THE LEGEND BEAST
Eris discovers her bond with the Eagle Legend Beast when the two meet in the Outlands. With Eris's intelligence and the Legend Beast's strength, they are a perfect fit.

Did you know?
The Eagle Legend Beast is a mother. She has two eggs in her nest in the Outlands, which Eris helps her rescue when they are stolen by the Outland Tribes.

Beak produces wild Eagle cry.

Blue and gold markings match the colors of the Eagle Tribe.

ERIS'S FIRE EAGLE FLYER

STREAMLINED JET

With the power of Fire CHI, Eris can fly faster than ever before in her Fire Eagle Flyer. Its flexible wings adjust to make the most of every swoop and dive, and its ice-melting blasters can take on the toughest—and coldest—opponents in all of Chima.

FIRE POWER

Eagles have never flown like this before! Powered by Fire CHI and with flames around the outside, the Flyer blazes through the sky like a comet. With able Eris in the pilot's seat, it's a tough bird to beat!

Wingtips adjust for optimal aerodynamics.

Fire markings show alliance with the Phoenix Tribe.

STEEP DIVE
Wings tucked back, beak slicing through the air, and fire missiles aimed and ready—the aerodynamic Eagle Flyer is at its fastest when diving toward its target.

Eris sits well back as her plane goes into a steep nose dive.

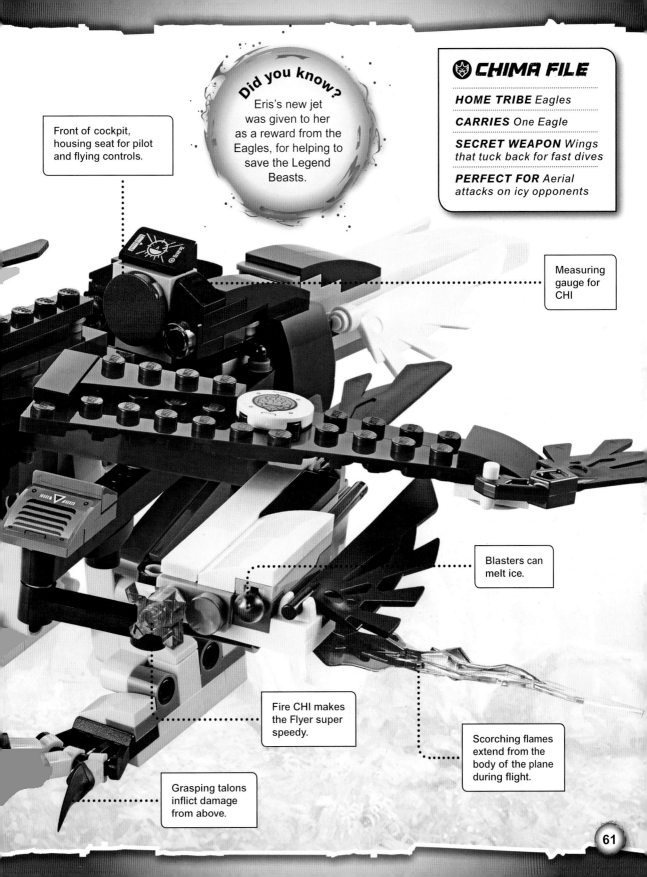

Front of cockpit, housing seat for pilot and flying controls.

CHIMA FILE

HOME TRIBE Eagles

CARRIES One Eagle

SECRET WEAPON Wings that tuck back for fast dives

PERFECT FOR Aerial attacks on icy opponents

Measuring gauge for CHI

Blasters can melt ice.

Fire CHI makes the Flyer super speedy.

Scorching flames extend from the body of the plane during flight.

Grasping talons inflict damage from above.

EAGLE TRIBE
WEAPONS
AERODYNAMIC EQUIPMENT

For the high-flying Eagle Tribe, the perfect weapons have to be lightweight, well-balanced, and easy to wield on the fly. This cool collection of spears, swords, and axes fits the bill, with some of the most advanced and aerodynamic fighting tools in all of Chima.

Did you know?
After use, all CHI-powered weapons need time to rest and regain their power.

Even with this massive weapon, Eris can fly with ease!

Sliver of crystal looks fragile but is incredibly sturdy.

ERIS'S GOLDEN HALOR STAFF
Eris is rewarded for her great skill and bravery with this Golden Halor Staff—headed by a razor-sharp ax blade and powered by CHI from below. The weapon is taller than an Eagle, but it is surprisingly light—great for zippy flyers like Eris!

CHI adds energy from the bottom up.

INFLIGHT MODE

Royal Valious of Unity

JABBING JABA

This modest staff isn't as elegant as most Eagle gear, but its strong, simple construction and ease of use make it a battle essential.

Jaba

TWIN POWER

The Royal Valious of Unity is the exact twin of the Lion's Royal Valious sword. It has long been a symbol of the pact between the Eagles and Lions to fight together for the good of Chima.

GOLDEN EGGOLA NUNCHUCKS

One wrong move and this chained weapon could knock the feathers right off its user—but in Eglor's expert talons, they'll find their target.

Eggola

EGLOR'S INVENTIONS

Jabahak

Lightnix

Trust Eglor's mathematical mind to design weapons so precisely balanced and shaped, that they slice through the air as easily as an Eagle wing. Eglor is pretty sure these weapons both have special powers, but his fellow Eagles aren't so sure!

GOLDEN WEAPONS

These golden weapons look like they'd weigh a ton—but each one is expertly made to be as light as a feather!

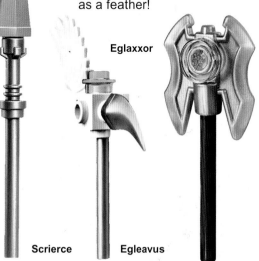

Eglaxxor

Scrierce

Egleavus

THE RAVEN TRIBE

Master thieves, the Ravens are out for one thing and one thing only, and that's a healthy profit. They are not prejudiced in who they steal from, targeting friends and foes alike in their quest for financial gain. Most of the other tribes agree that it's best to avoid the Ravens altogether— and if you don't, best check your pockets before leaving their company!

Razcal races away with stolen CHI on his Double Crosser vehicle.

RAZAR
PRINCE AMONG THIEVES

The wheeling-dealing Razar only has one thing on his mind—profit! Ravens are notoriously sneaky and greedy, and he is no exception. Razor has no scruples to ruffle his feathers. If he can sell stolen weapons or Speedorz back to their owners, he will.

WILY CHANCER
Razar will do anything to get his claws on Golden CHI, even compete in Speedor races in the hope of winning it. Not a natural rider, devious Razar relies on underhand tactics.

⬤ CHIMA FILE

LIKES Profit

DISLIKES Losses

BEST PAL Open to offers

ARCHENEMIES
Good guy know-it-all Laval

Shrewd expression

Straps and buckles handy for holding stolen goods

Hook for a hand (probably sold for profit or lost in a fight!)

Did you know?
Razar's weapon of choice is the Slizar—"donated" by the Wolves. Razar will not confirm or deny if his Slizar was to blame for his lost hand.

FAIR-WEATHER FRIEND
There's no honor among these thieves: Ravens have no close friends, not even amongst themselves. Razar happily makes temporary alliances with anyone, but only for as long as there's something in it for him.

CHI-POWERED
RAZAR
FEARSOME FIEND

Razar's CHI power-up moment reveals him to be a spectacular figure with massive, powerful wings. Good at thieving before, he's even better now, with added strength and power to fend off foes.

SEE THE DIFFERENCE
With CHI, Razar's wings split into six individual super-sized blades.

Sharp black and purple blades for wings

RARE SIGHT
Selling CHI brings in big profits, so Ravens only use it themselves as a last resort. But when needs must, a CHI Raven is an awesome combatant, with vicious razor-sharp bladed wings and super-strength.

Glowing red battle scythes

RAWZOM
GRAND THIEF MASTER

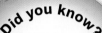
Did you know?
With his excellent eyesight, Rawzom can spy on other tribes—and spot thieving opportunities—from the skies high over Chima.

The leader of the Raven Tribe, Rawzom was never appointed or elected. Perhaps he bribed someone—or maybe just looked the part with his gold-plated gear! Although King, he's not above petty thievery when the mood strikes.

SELF-SERVING
Rawzom has his own personal interests at heart, and considers what's best for his tribe second. In the interests of feathering his own nest, he always has a profit-making scheme on the go.

⬥ CHIMA FILE

LIKES *Money-making plans*

DISLIKES *Losing out*

BEST PAL *Right-hand Raven, Razcal*

ARCHENEMIES *Whoever he is paid to attack*

As leader, Rawzom chooses a highly decorated helmet.

Keen-eyed gaze

Expensive golden armor

ROYAL STAFF
As well as being a mean attack staff, the Slashersekt is said to whisper wisdom to its bearer. Rawzom claims that it tells him he is the best Raven leader ever!

RAZCAL
MASTER MATHEMATICIAN

Razcal knows exactly where all the money is. As the Raven Tribe's respected accountant, he keeps a beady eye on all the Raven's wheeling and dealing. It's important work—the tribe's morale depends on his official count of their profits.

Cold and calculating expression

DOUBLE CROSSER
No ground is too rugged for Razcal in his all-terrain vehicle, aptly named the Double-Crosser. Speeding into the fray and out again, Razcal can "liberate" CHI before anyone has noticed.

⬡ CHIMA FILE

LIKES Counting money

DISLIKES Anything that isn't profit-related

BEST PAL His calculator

ARCHENEMIES Interruptors

Gold-plated prosthetic upper beak

Pouch contains stolen golden goods.

ALL-ROUNDER
Calculating Razcal is not just good with figures, he gets stuck into the business of grabbing swag too. As an expert pilot, he flies one of the Raven Tribe's precious gliders in daring CHI raids. The bottom line is: The more trinkets and treasure he can swipe, the more there is to tally up afterwards!

Golden Raven symbols

Did you know?
Razcal lends an air of respectability to the Ravens. Without him they'd be plain old thieves, but with him they are entrepreneurs.

RIZZO
LOWEST OF THE LOW

Although Ravens have few morals, they normally have a few standards. Not Rizzo. At the very bottom of the pack, this Raven is utterly shameless and has nicknamed himself the "Shah of Shamelessness."

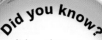

Did you know?
It is unknown how Rizzo lost his eye and leg, but it wouldn't be surprising if it was during a daredevil CHI raid or theft attempt.

BATTLE-SCARRED
When it comes to his crafty, criminal ways, Rizzo is all Raven. Unfortunately, the same cannot be said for his body. Scrapes and scuffles have taken their toll on his ravaged figure. Now part-bird, part-machinery, he has a replacement leg and metal eye patch. Not that this holds him back from plundering and pilfering.

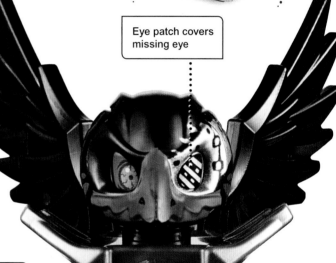

Eye patch covers missing eye

Rizzo still has use of both hands— for now.

Metal peg leg is not too much of a hindrance as Rizzo prefers to fly.

⬡ CHIMA FILE

LIKES *Profit at any cost*

DISLIKES *Not making money*

BEST PALS *Whoever pays him the most: Wolf, Croc, or Raven*

ARCHENEMIES *Eagles— only Ravens should have control of Chima's airspace*

GRAB AND GO
Rizzo's Grabbertus was designed specially for the Ravens. It extends with a simple click to snatch an object from a safe distance. It also retracts quickly, for a quick getaway.

RAZAR'S CHI RAIDER

FLYING TRASH CAN

Raven vehicles like the CHI Raider lack the grace of Eagle ones because they are loaded with hoarded junk. The plane itself is a well engineered, advanced piece of kit, but all that tat slows it down.

MAKESHIFT AMMO
The shrewd Ravens always know exactly what they have strapped to their vehicles, and the value of it. As a last resort, they can use the least valuable materials for bombardment.

Poised missiles

Sharp, grasping beak

Rear storage bay

FORWARD MOTION
The CHI Raider gains momentum from flapping wings, rather than jets. It also gains speed from turbines powered by the Ravens' CHI. Raven planes are made from a durable lightweight material, but, like most Raven objects, its origin is dubious.

Talons double as grappling hooks

🔷 CHIMA FILE

HOME TRIBE Ravens

CARRIES Two Ravens

SECRET WEAPON Jettisoned junk

PERFECT FOR Swooping in and stealing CHI

71

RAZCAL'S GLIDER
SWOOPING SPEEDSTER

This precious Raven Glider is swift and highly maneuverable. Reckless pilot Razcal uses it to swoop down on unsuspecting targets and grab their valuables before they have a chance to blink! Its wings can be spread wide for gliding or pulled in for sudden nose-dives.

FLYING FREE
The open-topped Glider may not offer much protection to the exposed pilot, but this doesn't faze Razcal. His favorite weapon, the Bulwark, makes the perfect protective shield—with the added bonus of firing CHI pulses.

Maneuverable wings

BALL AND CHAIN
Swinging low from the back of the Glider is a grabber on a long chain, used for snatching stolen goods. It can also tangle up pursuers long enough for Razcal to make his getaway—or capture them for ransom if needs be!

CHI glows red when used for theft!

Sharp pointed beak

Stolen CHI

Assault chain snatches CHI.

Grasping talons

💎 CHIMA FILE

HOME TRIBE Ravens

CARRIES One Raven

SECRET WEAPON Swinging ball and chain

PERFECT FOR Speedy CHI raids

RAVEN WEAPONS

"BORROWED" GADGETS

FOR FIGHTING AND STEALING

Rawzom's Slashersekt

Thundax

STOLEN GOODS
The Slashersekt is the only weapon of genuine Raven origin. The others have elements suspiciously reminiscent of Eagle and Wolf weapons—amongst others.

Razar's Slizar

"STICK 'EM UP"
Rizzo covers all bases with this part-blaster, part-ax. If the pulse beam fails, he can attack his enemy with the red blade.

Snypax

Bazooclaw

RIZZO'S BAZOOCLAW
With a claw borrowed from the Wolf blacksmith and a sonar disc borrowed from the Eagles, this is a nifty little weapon.

Vengjacked

HIJACKED VENGJACKED
The Ravens will swear blind that the "Vengjacked" has been theirs for generations even though it's clearly the Crocodiles' Vengious of Honor.

Bokraw

UP TO NO GOOD
Razcal's latest weapon is a multipurpose mix of technology.

THE WOLF TRIBE

Cunning and fierce, the battle-hungry Wolves never shy away from a fight—and they always seem to have a bone to pick with someone. Their roving lifestyle gives them plenty of chances to make enemies. Among themselves though, there's almost never disagreement. Their Wolf-pack mentality means they think and act as a unit.

Wakz cuts a mean figure, racing through the forest on his trike.

WORRIZ
LEADER OF THE PACK

Like all Wolves, Worriz is best at following instinct and serving the pack—not being nice to the neighbors. Nevertheless, he answers the call to represent his fellow Wolves when needed, signing treaties and keeping the peace with other tribes.

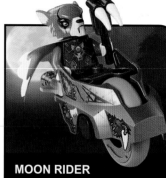

MOON RIDER
With a tooth-tipped battle ax by his side, Worriz rides high on his fanged Speedor. Once a month, the full moon gives Wolves an extra burst of energy!

TOP DOG
Worriz isn't your average diplomat—he is fearless and ruthless, but he is the best the Wolf Tribe has to offer. His toughness serves him well in battle and when traveling off the beaten track, and he is always working for the good of the pack.

🐺 CHIMA FILE

LIKES Meat (Lions are said to be very tasty)

DISLIKES Interference from other tribes

BEST PAL
Worriz loves only Worriz

ARCHENEMIES
All other tribes

Jagged cape gives Worriz a wild-yet-regal appearance.

Animal tail trophy torn from unfortunate foe.

Did you know?
Rude, short-tempered Worriz was chosen as the Wolves' representative because he was voted "most personable."

CHI-POWERED
WORRIZ
FEARSOME AND FERAL

Worriz's Power Warrior towers over all others when powered by CHI—or speeds by in a blur, running on his ultra-fast legs. Worriz is even fiercer than usual when fighting for the pack with this super-strong warrior spirit!

Spiky shoulder guards won't let danger come too close.

Glowing red eyes reveal malicious intent.

Giant paws strike at enemies or hold supercharged weapons.

LONE WOLF
A burst of CHI in his breastplate releases an extension of Worriz's raw animalistic powers. If he seemed wild before, he's all beast now!

Razor-edged shield offers defense and offense in one.

SEE THE DIFFERENCE
Worriz's normal body looks tiny beside his monstrous CHI-powered frame!

Sword glows red with CHI.

WINZAR
FEARLESS FOOT SOLDIER

It's clear just by looking at battle-scarred Winzar that this Wolf is not afraid of a fight. He'll jump into a battle for the smallest reason, no matter the risks. Winzar's claws are ready—but his strategic skills could use some sharpening up!

Painful blood-red scar is a relic of battles past.

An angry snarl is how Winzar says hello.

Winzar's fur is scruffy and unkempt.

WOLF GLIDER
With four skis for maximum maneuverability, this speedy machine races into the fray—because the only thing more fearsome than Winzar is Winzar approaching at high speeds!

WILD SIDE
With Winzar, what you see is what you get: wild, mean, marked by past battles... but always ready for the next one! Winzar doesn't like anything remotely fussy, so his clothes are as simple as possible, and his manners are short and gruff too.

Did you know?
A run-in with someone's claw left Winzar with only one eye. However, he only needs the one to know when he doesn't like what he sees!

WILHURT
HEARTLESS HUNTER

It's right there in the name—this crazed guy will hurt anyone who crosses his path! Wilhurt's job is to help Worriz—but his passion is attacking anything and everything that moves. To keep him from going completely berserk, it's best to keep him occupied.

MEAN MACHINE
Wilhurt is just as crazy on wheels as he is on his paws! On his maniacal motorcycle, Wilhurt chases down enemies with terrifying speed—look out for those mighty tires approaching!

Did you know?
If Wilhurt goes too long without hurting someone, he starts to really lose control! It's best to keep away when he's in one of those moods.

Crazed toothy smile and narrowed yellow eyes are signs that Wilhurt is about to get into trouble!

 **CHIMA FILE**

LIKES Fighting, hunting

DISLIKES Sitting still

BEST PAL Winzar, if he must choose somebody

ARCHENEMY Everyone in sight

Unusual black fur means Wilhurt can easily sneak up on others in the dark.

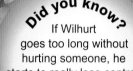

CHI medallion hangs from a cord around Wilhurt's neck.

Belt is filled with trophies from past victories.

DARK MOTIVES
Looking at Wilhurt's fang-covered belt, menacing smile, and seriously scary eyes, you might get the impression he's up to no good. You would be right! For Wilhurt, any moment not spent causing havoc is a moment wasted.

WINDRA

TECH-WHIZ

The cunning and creative Windra doesn't take any nonsense. She's in her element tinkering with a Wolf vehicle to make it even faster, tougher, and meaner, or driving one of them in search of an enemy to attack!

WHIRLY WOLF
When the Wolves work together, they can do anything—even launch their non-flying tribe off the ground! Windra played a key role in the invention of this dual-bladed helicopter, and is an expert at flying it.

Did you know?
Windra keeps two long daggers strapped to her back at all times... just in case.

This expression seems calm, but means, "Don't mess with me."

🐺 CHIMA FILE

LIKES *Working on vehicles*

DISLIKES *Worriz's unwelcome attentions*

BEST PALS *A wrench and a broken engine*

ARCHENEMY *Worriz, Worriz, Worriz*

CHI medallion is designed with four sharp points and strung on a necklace.

PRETTY SCARY
Windra's good looks may charm Worriz, but the traits he finds irresistible—violence, cruelty, non-stop snarling—to others seem just plain scary.

White cape trails dramatically on high-speed rides.

Elaborate full-body armor, complete with canine detailing

WAKZ
WISE WOLF ELDER

Top dog Wakz has been around longer than any other Wolf, but despite his age, he's never lost his edge. In this tough tribe, anyone who survives to Wakz's ripe old age has to be fierce, cunning, and strong. This experienced warrior is all of that, and more!

GRAYBEARD
The years have added touches of silver to Wakz's dark gray coat, but it's easy to see in his narrowed eyes that he's never lost an ounce of ferocity. If anything, he's become fiercer over the years as he's fine-tuned the arts of intimidation and warfare.

Patches of lighter gray show Wakz's age.

Beware his steely gaze.

Jagged patterns cover Wakz's tunic.

Teeth strung to leg band. Whose teeth? No one knows.

MAKING WAKZ TRACKS
Just because Wakz has been around a while doesn't mean he's slowing down. His super-sleek Speedor tears by in a bright-red flash!

Did you know?
Wakz has been known to throw an unfair punch from time to time. When it comes to winning, he does whatever it takes!

WAKZ'S
PACK TRACKER
POWERFUL RAIDER

For quick attacks or CHI raids, the Wolves can rely on Wakz's Pack Tracker. With plant-trampling wheels and a blasting cannon capable of starting a forest fire, it's designed to get through Chima's thickest jungles with terrifying ease.

TAIL END
Flailing behind the Pack Tracker, a toothed tail smashes and destroys as it swings— watch out, Equila! It's also useful for hauling the Tracker out of a tight spot if it gets stuck.

Cannon blasts through roadblocks

Burner leaves a trail of fire in its wake

Chained tail swings from the rear bumper

SMASH AND GRAB
With a huge, dense frame and powerful engine, this wagon was not built for stealth missions! But for breaking and entering, stealing CHI, and rushing away again, there's no vehicle better suited.

Off-road suspension for covering rocky ground

Claw and fang attachments slice away vines and brush at ground level.

🐺 CHIMA FILE

HOME TRIBE Wolves

CARRIES Two co-pilots

SECRET WEAPON Jungle smashing abilities

PERFECT FOR CHI raids

WOLF
LEGEND BEAST
WILD THING

The super-tough, extra-mean, never-back-down Wolves have one soft spot: They are completely devoted to their Legend Beast. The lithe, powerful Beast represents everything the pack values, such as fighting instincts and cunning.

TWO PEAS IN A POD
Like the other Legend Beasts, the Wolf has a special connection with her tribe. She lets Worriz ride on her back, and he is the only Wolf who can interpret her howl.

Powerful haunches bear the symbol of the Wolf Tribe.

Wide mouth for howling at the moon

Four-legged walk remained, without CHI to change it.

🐺 CHIMA FILE

LIKES Wolf Tribe rescuers

DISLIKES Poison given to her by the Scorpions

BEST PAL Worriz

ARCHENEMIES Bats, Scorpions, Spiders

Sharp claws make every paw a mighty weapon.

RUNNING FREE
Having never been transformed by CHI, or civilized by life in Chima, the Wolf Legend Beast retains her natural lupine instincts. In fact, life in the wild Outlands has helped her to become even more powerful, and her howl is fiercer than ever!

83

WORRIZ'S COMBAT LAIR
WOLF HQ ON WHEELS

Perfect for the roving Wolves, their mobile headquarters keeps their high-tech battle capabilities on the move. When manned by a whole team of wolves, it's an intimidating unit, but like a real wolf pack, it can also split up to track and capture prey.

MULTIFUNCTIONAL MACHINE
A moving wolf muzzle gives the Combat Lair a predatory look—just right for the attacking Wolf Tribe. But that's not the only threat onboard this massive machine: Five vehicles and a mobile prison can break off into individual attack vehicles to cover the battlefield.

Fanged Wolf mouth opens and closes.

Angled bumper for ploughing through dense undergrowth.

Smaller front wheels of detachable bikes

Massive wheels keep this huge machine moving.

🐺 CHIMA FILE

HOME TRIBE Wolves

CARRIES The whole pack

SECRET WEAPON
Five vehicles in one

PERFECT FOR Keeping
the tribe on the move

Rear wheels
rotate for
use with the
motorcycle.

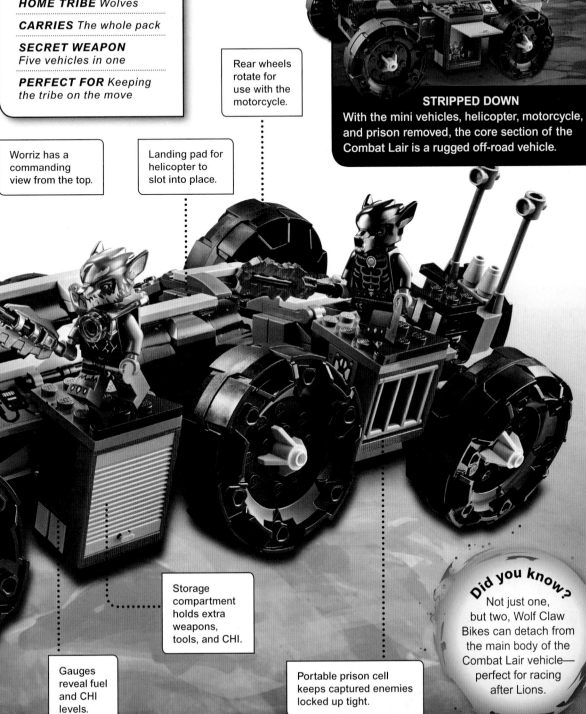

STRIPPED DOWN
With the mini vehicles, helicopter, motorcycle,
and prison removed, the core section of the
Combat Lair is a rugged off-road vehicle.

Worriz has a
commanding
view from the top.

Landing pad for
helicopter to
slot into place.

Storage
compartment
holds extra
weapons,
tools, and CHI.

Gauges
reveal fuel
and CHI
levels.

Portable prison cell
keeps captured enemies
locked up tight.

Did you know?
Not just one,
but two, Wolf Claw
Bikes can detach from
the main body of the
Combat Lair vehicle—
perfect for racing
after Lions.

WOLF TRIBE
WEAPONS
TEETH AND CLAWS

The Wolf Tribe doesn't need fancy add-ons or high-tech mumbo-jumbo: jagged edges and heavy handles suit them just fine. Simply give this battle-loving group some basic axes and clubs, and they'll show that the power of the pack can make any weapon dangerous!

Did you know?
The fang-shaped spikes in the Wolves' weapons aren't actual fangs—they're made from super-tough chimoralium.

CHI Dirimous

CHI gives off non Wolf-like blue glow.

WORRIZ'S NEW KIT
Worriz gets a whole new glow when his Outlands weapons pulse blue with positive CHI energy. His willingness to work alongside past enemies for the good of Chima proves that his intentions are not all evil! The shape and size of his new blade is a lot like traditional Wolf weapons, but more advanced and powerful.

New golden armor

Translucent shield is lightweight but extra tough.

WOLF WARFARE

TO THE POINT

The pack fights as one, so most of its weapons look pretty similar. Most are fairly simple, too—jagged edges and simple designs show the Wolves don't care much about decorative details. As long as their weapons can be used to smash and slash, the Wolves are happy!

CHI
Jahak

Vengious
of Honor

VENGIOUS OF HONOR

This Croc blade was a gift from King Crominus, in thanks for the Wolves' promise of loyalty in an oath known as the Pledge of the Pack. Like the Pledge itself, the Vengious can't be destroyed.

Slizar

Diremptior

ARMED AND DANGEROUS

DOUBLE TROUBLE

For the low-tech Wolves, the Maulus is unusually thoughtful in its design. The two fangs symbolize how the pack acts as one, striking at exactly the same time. They're also a tribute to the Mother Wolf.

Dirimous

WILL HURT MORE

No one needs a weapon to cause mayhem less than Wilhurt, but this CHI-powered blade certainly leaves a mark.

Maulus

Howlorr

SHARP SHOOTER

Windra has a gift for tinkering, so it's no surprise she has one of the Wolf Tribe's most advanced weapons—a CHI blaster that can cause damage from a great distance.

THE GORILLA TRIBE

Spreading a message of peace and harmony, the Gorillas just want to live and let live. Seeking a state of existence called "The Great Mellow," this tribe isn't that interested in power games. Which is just as well, as they are easily the strongest and most formidable warriors in all of Chima. When combat is called for, their opponents had better watch out!

Gorzan wields his Tree Tumbler weapon whilst riding his golden Speedor.

GORZAN
GENTLE GIANT

Gorzan is one of the most caring animals in all of Chima. When it comes to brute strength, he is big and strong enough to beat almost any enemy in a fight—but he always worries afterwards about any flowers he might have stepped on in the heat of battle.

🦍 CHIMA FILE

LIKES Nature, the world around him

DISLIKES Litterers

BEST PAL Anyone who says "hi" to him!

ARCHENEMIES Nature haters

Did you know?
Gorzan is so concerned for his fellow Gorillas' feelings that he doesn't like to label himself a leader—in case it offends others.

Mellow gaze

SENSITIVE SOUL
After defeating an opponent, Gorzan immediately feels guilty about any pain he may have caused. The truth is Gorzan would much rather chill out and pick nits out of your fur than fight you!

CHI Dentmakor

Fierce war paint stripes

Dark brown armor for camouflaging with Chima's forests.

TEMPER TANTRUMS
Although Gorzan is laid-back, he does have a competitive side. He is often heard crying in frustration when he is defeated in Speedorz races.

Sturdy limbs like tree trunks

CHI-POWERED GORZAN
PRIZE FIGHTER

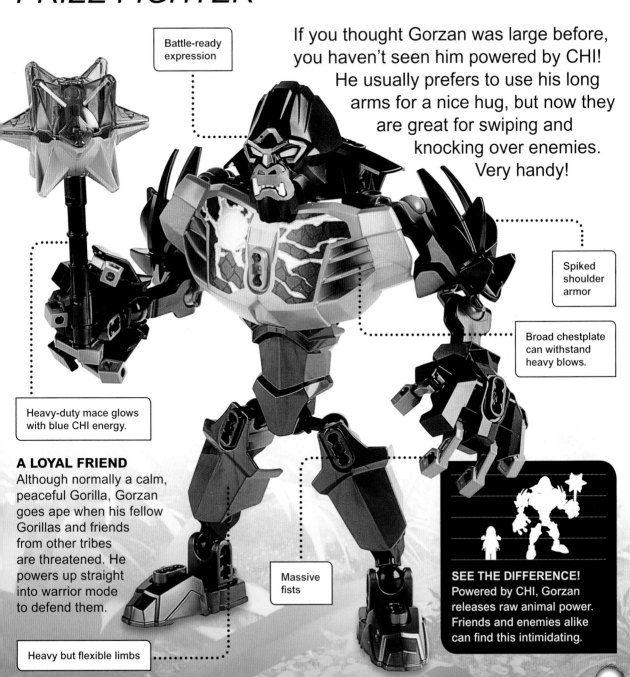

Battle-ready expression

If you thought Gorzan was large before, you haven't seen him powered by CHI! He usually prefers to use his long arms for a nice hug, but now they are great for swiping and knocking over enemies. Very handy!

Spiked shoulder armor

Broad chestplate can withstand heavy blows.

Heavy-duty mace glows with blue CHI energy.

A LOYAL FRIEND
Although normally a calm, peaceful Gorilla, Gorzan goes ape when his fellow Gorillas and friends from other tribes are threatened. He powers up straight into warrior mode to defend them.

Massive fists

SEE THE DIFFERENCE!
Powered by CHI, Gorzan releases raw animal power. Friends and enemies alike can find this intimidating.

Heavy but flexible limbs

G'LOONA
BUDDING ADVENTURER

Little orphan G'Loona is a young Gorilla who just wants to join in with Gorzan's grand adventures. She looks up to him and is always trying to tag along on his missions with his friends. However, instead of helping, G'Loona usually ends up needing to be saved herself.

 **CHIMA FILE**

LIKES *Being a part of things*

DISLIKES *Being left out*

BEST PAL *Gorzan*

ARCHENEMIES *Any enemy of Gorzan*

G'Loona decorates her head and body with purple flowers. Like all Gorillas, she loves nature.

GORZAN'S SHADOW
G'Loona loves Gorzan like a big brother, and he loves her too—but wishes she would just stay at home and out of trouble! Maybe someday, G'Loona might be the one to save his hide in return.

STILL LIFE
G'Loona fancies herself as an artist and loves to draw. She practices painting her favorite things—bananas!

Toothy grin

G'Loona wishes to be treated like an adult Gorilla, but her short stature reveals her true age.

Did you know?
G'Loona is inspired by strong female role models, such as Eris the Eagle.

GRUMLO
CHILLED-OUT LEADER

As one of the Gorilla Tribe's elders, Grumlo helps set the tone for the whole tribe's philosophy—ultra laid-back and groovy, man! But that doesn't mean that Grumlo can't step up when the going gets tough.

PARTY ANIMAL
After fighting battles, the Gorillas like to join their allies like Laval and Eris to celebrate. Even Grumlo can be seen joining in the fun!

Painted Gorilla Tribe New Age markings.

Wrinkles display both age and wisdom.

YOGA GURU
Grumlo can wield several weapons at once in battle, thanks to his advanced yoga skills. The flexible fighter can turn a graceful stretch into a lightning-fast punch and he is always one step ahead of the enemy. Mellow Grumlo would rather be munching on some granola though!

Gray fur of silverback Gorilla.

Hidden banana tucked into belt

Strong feet for climbing trees and fighting enemies

🦍 CHIMA FILE

LIKES Yoga

DISLIKES Disharmony

BEST PALS Everyone, dude!

ARCHENEMIES No one

93

GRIZZAM
COMPETITIVE SPEED DEMON

Confident Grizzam loves to stand out—his unique snowy white fur sets him apart from his fellow tribe members. Little is known about this mysterious Gorilla, but everyone agrees that he is a powerful warrior and a spectacular sight on his transparent Speedor!

JUNGLE CHALLENGE
Driven Grizzam competes in the Gorilla Tribe contest. He wants to hit the target harder than anyone else, in order to win CHI.

WACKY WARRIOR
Whether he is chasing down Crocodiles for cutting down flowers, or going head-to-head with Wolves in battle, Grizzam is one competitive Gorilla warrior. The only downside to his talent for fighting is that his distinctive fur is easy to spot in the jungle!

Uncompromising expression

Vines criss-crossing body hold CHI in place

Powerful Gorilla physique

Bright white fur

🦍 CHIMA FILE

LIKES *Being different*

DISLIKES *Losing, socializing*

BEST PALS *Fellow Gorillas*

ARCHENEMY *Cragger, for the damage he has done to nature*

Did you know?
Just like Laval and Cragger, Grizzam's favorite Speedor Champion is the Peacock racer Dom de la Woosh!

GORILLA LEGEND BEAST
FEROCIOUS PROTECTOR

CHIMA FILE

LIKES *Bananas, fighting*

DISLIKES *Stepping on plants*

BEST PAL *Gorzan*

ARCHENEMIES *Outland Tribes*

As one of the first Legend Beasts to be discovered in the Outlands, it is the Gorilla Legend Beast who helps to prove that the Legend is true. Full of surprises, this creature is as powerful as he looks, but also very mellow!

Snarling face terrifies Scorpions, Bats, and Spiders alike.

Gorzan hitches a lift to ride into battle.

POWERFUL CONNECTION
The Legend Beast helps to enhance Gorzan's powers whenever he is in its presence. Gorzan becomes stronger than ever, even more nature-loving, and super chilled out. Groovy!

Broad and sturdy chest

Tribal markings

TO THE RESCUE
After springing to save the band of heroes several times, the helpful Gorilla Legend Beast is always ready to agree to help defeat the sinister Outland Tribes.

Strong fingers for gripping and climbing.

GORZAN'S GORILLA STRIKER

MIGHTY MECH

When the Gorillas' fleet of Gorilla Strikers swings through the forest, it is an awesome sight to behold. Gorzan's Striker is a mean, keen fighting machine—it's best to stay out of its way if you don't want to be pelted with flying fruit!

RESCUE MISSION

Gorzan's custom-made mech has seen some action in its time. When naughty Rizzo kidnapped G'Loona, Gorzan battered his Raven nest with the Striker's missiles and used its long arms to knock the crook straight off his perch.

CHIMA FILE

HOME TRIBE *Gorillas*

HOLDS *One Gorilla*

SECRET WEAPON *Banana missiles*

PERFECT FOR *Swinging through the swamp after Crocodiles*

Rapid-fire banana missile

Broad shoulders are as wide as a tree.

Hydraulic hoses flow CHI from source to limbs.

CHI-powered chest missiles

Flexible joints

Extendable fingers for grasping weapons and swatting foes.

Gorilla Tribe symbols

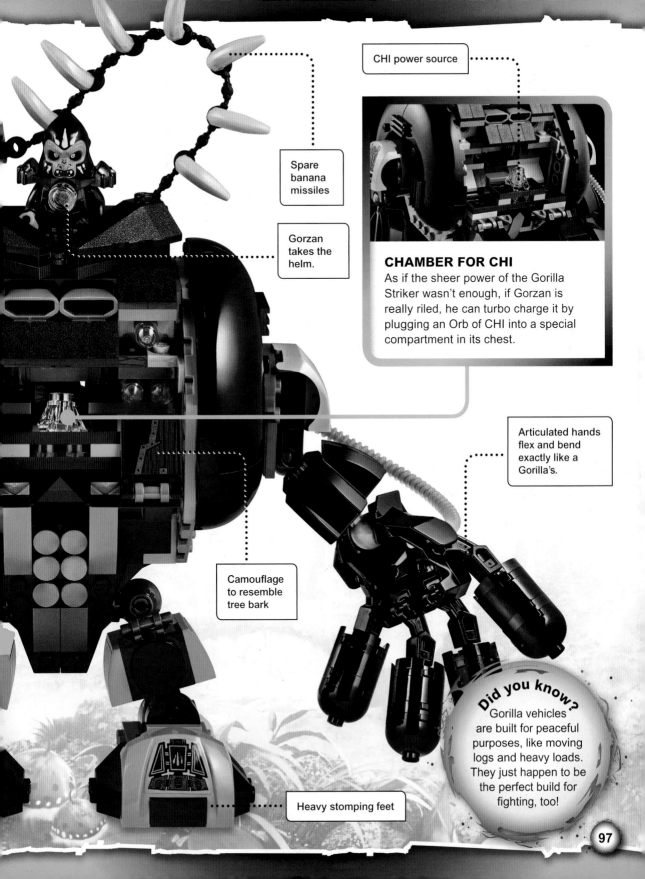

CHI power source

Spare banana missiles

Gorzan takes the helm.

CHAMBER FOR CHI

As if the sheer power of the Gorilla Striker wasn't enough, if Gorzan is really riled, he can turbo charge it by plugging an Orb of CHI into a special compartment in its chest.

Articulated hands flex and bend exactly like a Gorilla's.

Camouflage to resemble tree bark

Heavy stomping feet

Did you know?
Gorilla vehicles are built for peaceful purposes, like moving logs and heavy loads. They just happen to be the perfect build for fighting, too!

GORILLA TRIBE
WEAPONS
JUST BANANAS!

The Gorillas would rather live and let live, man. But when their peace is threatened, they are ready and armed with devastating weapons. These have features that remind the Gorillas of their favorite things, such as bananas, or look similar to themselves, with huge Gorilla fists.

FRUITY FUN
Gorzan's favorite weapon is a Banana Buster, which is an upgraded Cudgellor Club with added banana detailing. The fist part of the club now extends on a spring, while the bananas pop out and cause messy chaos— and a tasty battle snack!

Armor upgraded from brown to silver

Dual banana attachment

Fist Club

Sturdy base and grip for quirky attachments

HAMMERS

Gorillas like to carry simple weapons to protect nature against those who don't pay it enough respect. These hammers are forged by the Gorilla blacksmith in the jungle treetops, primarily as defensive weapons.

Dentmakor

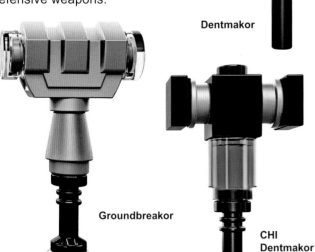

Groundbreakor

CHI Dentmakor

AXES

A double-ended ax is perfect for hand-to-hand combat. Alternatively, the blunt stone-carved hammer staff is traditionally a decorative accessory, but it can be used as a weapon if needed.

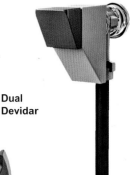

Dual Devidar

Tree Tumbler

OVERSIZED WEAPONS

FIT LIKE GLOVES
G'Loona prefers to wear these oversized gauntlets, which she uses to pummel her enemies into submission.

Gamorette Gauntlets

Cudgellor

CUDGELLOR CLUB
Gorzan's original Cudgellor Club is simply an oversized hammer—perfect for fighting off crafty Crocs or wily Wolves when they threaten Gorzan's favorite flowers.

THE RHINO TRIBE

Not the brightest of the tribes, the Rhinos are short-sighted and clumsy. Because they are so simple-minded, they are easy targets for the crafty Crocs and the sly Ravens, who use them for their own ends. What they lack in brains, the Rhinos make up for with brawn—ramming and smashing, like bulls in a china shop. When they are not fighting, they are content to devote their time and energy to their "pet" rocks.

Rogon uses his powerful Rock Flinger vehicle to search for his pet rock!

ROGON
THICK SKIN, LITTLE BRAIN

Like others in the Rhino Tribe, Rogon is not the sharpest tool in the box. He barely knows where he is most of the time, but he does like to have fun. Lovestruck Rogon harbors a not-so-secret crush on Eris the Eagle, and his favorite things in the world are his pet rocks.

Patched-up broken horn

TWO WHEELER
If Rogon needs to go on a quick mission he takes his bike. Most of its power comes from the oversized rear CHI wheel— and a Rhino head frontage to strike fear into any enemies Rogon encounters.

PART OF THE ACTION
Rogon and the other Rhinos don't really understand the politics of Chima. Instead, they see battles as sport, and are happy to get involved and use up some of their energy in the rough and tumble of the disputes between other tribes. Most of the time, Rogon is content to do whatever Cragger tells him to do!

Gray rock-colored armor plating

Did you know?
Rhinos have terrible memories, so no one knows who is king. Rogon thinks he is from a "fancy" family, so that's good enough to make him number one!

🐾 CHIMA FILE

LIKES Rocks, partying

DISLIKES Killjoys

BEST PAL Eris the Eagle

ARCHENEMIES
Whoever Cragger reminds him to dislike

RINONA
BRIGHT SPARK

Unlike the dim-witted males of the Rhino Tribe, Rinona is intelligent. Brave too, she stows away to the Outlands with Rogon in an attempt to keep him safe and out of trouble. Her rash actions can cause trouble—Eris mistakes Rinona for Rogon's girlfriend, rather than his sister!

CLUMSY CLICHÉ
Rhinos are notoriously clumsy, mainly due to their bad eyesight. They're always falling over things, and each other, because they can't see clearly, and because their bodies are so large and unwieldy.

Studded CHI harness

Did you know?
Rogon can't remember who his parents were, but Rinona can. He relies on her to remember all the important stuff—like family members' birthdays.

Unusual purple markings on face

 **CHIMA FILE**

LIKES Protecting her big brother

DISLIKES Dumb Rhino clichés

BEST PAL Rogon

ARCHENEMIES Eris the Eagle

BRAINY BUNCH
It is not understood why the female Rhinos are more intelligent than the males, but it's just as well, for Rinona's brain power has often made up for Rogon's shortfall. And yet, in the presence of the Rhino Legend Beast, Rogon becomes a veritable genius—putting his sister quite to shame!

Wrinkled hide for surviving the roughest of fights and the harshest of tumbles.

103

ROGON'S
ROCK FLINGER
CHUNKY CHARIOT

Somewhat like its owner, the Rock Flinger is heavy and clumsy in a fight, but it is plated with thick armor and a catapult that Rogon fondly calls his "Boulder Boomer." However, when it comes to traveling fast and light, this is definitely not the machine to choose—as Rogon refuses to go anywhere without a heavy supply of spare boulders!

Rogon steers from the front.

"Eyes" glow blue with power of CHI to intimidate foes.

Battering ram "Hammer Horn" is shaped like a Rhino horn for bulldozing foes.

OUTLANDS MISSION
When eight representatives from the Tribes of Chima set off to the Outlands to find the Legend Beasts, they are not best pleased when Rogon insists on bringing his rock-filled tank. And yet, its impenetrable armor, sturdy form, and brutal weapons have got the team out of many tight spots. It even has space for Rinona to stowaway and join in on her brother's exciting adventure!

Heavy duty armor plating like thick Rhino hide

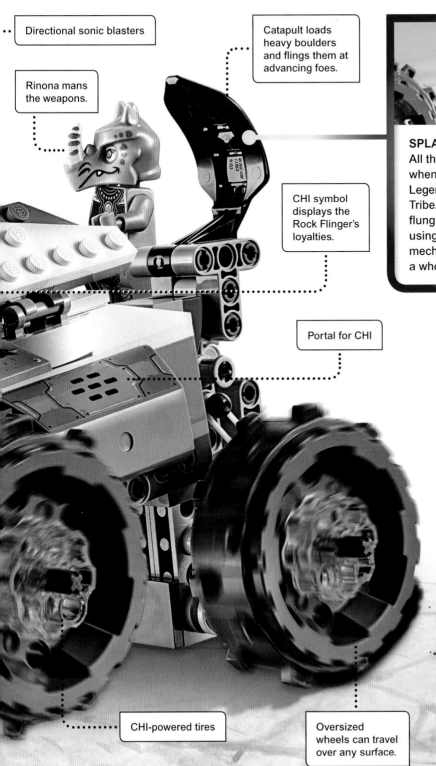

Directional sonic blasters

Rinona mans the weapons.

Catapult loads heavy boulders and flings them at advancing foes.

CHI symbol displays the Rock Flinger's loyalties.

Portal for CHI

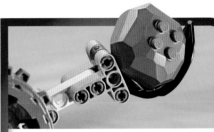

SPLAT-APULT
All those rocks come in handy when used to free the Rhino Legend Beast from the Spider Tribe. The heavy boulders can be flung from the powerful catapult using a complex, rock-powered mechanism—and can squash a whole Spider flat!

 **CHIMA FILE**

HOME TRIBE Rhino

CARRIES Rogon and Rinona, plus extra rocks

SECRET WEAPON Boulder catapult

PERFECT FOR Ramming and smashing

Did you know?
In order to rescue the Gorilla Legend Beast, Chima's heroes disguise the Rock Flinger to look like a giant fly to distract the Spiders!

CHI-powered tires

Oversized wheels can travel over any surface.

RHINO TRIBE WEAPONS

EASY DOES IT

Rhino weapons feature what Rhinos like best: hefty boulders and sharp horns! Rhinos are incredibly short-sighted and not that bright, so their weapons are large and easy to wield. The Rhinoceros style of fighting is all about ramming and smashing, so their weapons reflect this—pure power, rather than complex tactics and fancy features.

CHI shield

Heavy hammer built from rock

ROGON'S RAMMER SLAMMER
Combining a heavy rock with a sharp horn, Rogon's hammer is extra powerful when powered up by CHI. Rogon's new weapon doesn't require him to think too hard, which is just as well—it hurts his brain too much! Now Rogon is well equipped to take on giant Spiders in the Outlands.

Bulky and strong silver armor

BULLDOZING BLASTER

Extra-large white Rhino horn

Boulder Boomer

ROGON'S EXTRA STEADY BOULDER BOOMER

Rogon's most impressive weapon is an oversized blaster with counterbalances on either side of the muzzle to make aiming extra easy. Shooting this weapon is really simple—even for a Rhino like Rogon.

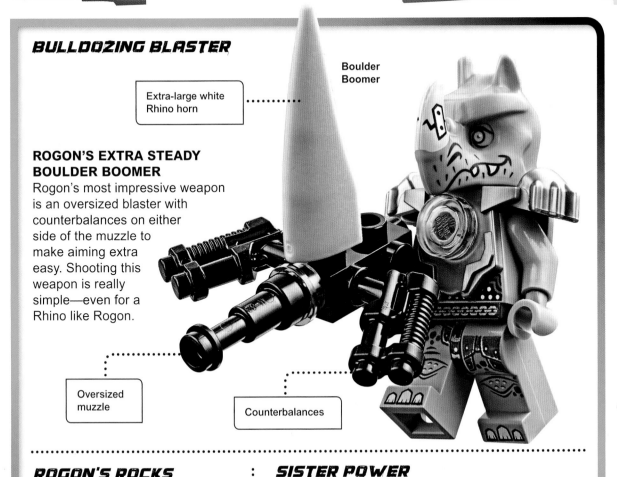

Oversized muzzle

Counterbalances

ROGON'S ROCKS

LANDSLIDE!

The Rhinos' favorite weapons are also their pets! Rocks are special to the Rhinos, and are easy to fling at the enemy in battle with the Rhinos' super strength. But they have to remember to retrieve them after the battle—or else they become very upset!

Boulder

SISTER POWER

The Hammerhorn

RINONA'S HAMMERHORN

Rinona's Hammerhorn is similar to Rogon's Rammer Slammer, but without the shield. It can be given extra power by plugging in a CHI crystal.

THE NOMADS

While most animals in Chima live in tribes, a few choose a solo life. Usually the only one of their kind, they turn up at major events and play a role in proceedings from time to time. But for the most part, these solitary souls prefer a quiet life away from the pomp and politics of Chima's main tribes.

Skinnet and Furty jump their Speedorz over obstacles on the race track.

FURTY
LONE RANGER

Furty the Fox's quick fingers have a talent for stealing. It's rumored that he is an uncanny impressionist, but his good heart usually keeps him from being too mean. Still, he can be convinced to play sneaky tricks—
if the price is right.

FAST FOX
Furty likes to keep to himself, but always turns up at the Speedor races, where he's easy to spot in his bright orange Speedor! Alternatively, he might be found causing trouble off the track.

PATCHED UP
Young orphan Furty has nobody to look out for him. He gets by on his own. His patched-together outfit is travel-worn, but perfect for him. Layers of different fabric and a loose neck tie ensure he's equipped for any weather, terrain, or mission!

Sly eyes are usually looking for ways to cause mischief.

Brown clothing works as protection and camouflage.

Knotted rope functions as a makeshift belt.

Did you know?
Furty the Fox is a distant cousin of those other canine troublemakers—the Wolves.

⊙ CHIMA FILE

LIKES Making mischief

DISLIKES Being shortchanged

BEST PAL Furty prefers his own company

ARCHENEMY Anyone he is paid to dislike

SKINNET
ODOROUS ALLY

Skinnet the Skunk doesn't mean any harm, but his stinks can break up a party! This good-natured guy tries to be sensitive to the noses of his friends, so he mainly stays on the outskirts of Chima—but he would love to have more pals to hang out with.

Spear powered by CHI, with extra-sharp plant attachments.

SPEEDY SKUNK
One place lonely Skinnet is allowed to join in the action is on the Speedor track. His smell's not so bad when he's rushing by at high speed on his black-and-white Speedor!

⊙ CHIMA FILE

LIKES Being around others

DISLIKES His own smell

BEST PAL Everyone, especially Laval and Eris

ARCHENEMY Peaceful Skinnet dislikes no one

Nose pink with embarrassment

Shy smile follows one of his jokes—or an accidental bad smell.

Vines from Skinnet's woodland home

WHAT A STINK
Skinnet makes the best of a smelly situation, turning his skills to his advantage. As neither good nor bad tribes want him around for long, he acts as negotiator, going between groups to resolve disputes. Although he longs to be a central part of a team, Skinnet masks his disappointment with an upbeat and cheery personality.

Did you know?
Chima used to be home to a whole tribe of Skunks, but they have long gone. Skinnet is the only one to have been seen—or smelt—since.

THE OUTLAND TRIBES

Deep in the dark and dangerous Outlands, amongst the poisonous plants, live the Bat, Spider, and Scorpion Tribes. These creepy crawlies were "created" when Laval accidently dropped CHI into the Gorge of Eternal Depth. Having made their way to the uncharted territory of the Outlands, these three tribes remain desperate for the power of CHI. The Spiders are master engineers and builders, and lead the assault on Chima. The vicious Scorpions add a sinister edge to the army, while the low-ranking Bats bulk up the vile and dangerous mass!

Predator Plants are capable of eating animals whole— including Blista the Bat!

BRAPTOR
MEAN FLYING MUSCLE

As one of the toughest of the Bats, Braptor enjoys going around hitting things aimlessly, including other Bats. Happy to be one of the crowd, Braptor uses brute strength to attack in an overwhelming mass.

Incredibly sensitive hearing

BRAPTOR'S WING STRIKER
This high speed, compact aircraft can produce a smokescreen that looks like a black cloud. It has a powerful blaster and flapping wings for use in attack. The strikers are also used to transport the Spiders to Mount Cavora.

Did you know?
The Bat Wing Strikers are powered by CHI, so Braptor must steal CHI from the Chima Tribes in order to power his vehicle.

Flexible wings poised for takeoff.

LISTENING IN
Although blind, Braptor has exceptional hearing and can hear conversations many miles away. This would make him an excellent spy, if only he had the brains to use this incredible skill to his advantage.

Strong, muscular physique

Claws for hanging upside down off branches

◎ CHIMA FILE

LIKES *Being part of the crowd*

DISLIKES *Thinking too much*

BEST PAL *Blista*

ARCHENEMIES *Chima's "heroes"*

BLISTA
TOP BAT WARRIOR

Blista is one of the fastest and strongest of the Bat Tribe, but he is also the most unreliable! He'd rather be playing pranks than fighting a battle, but if the rest of his Tribe is involved, then he's more than happy to tag along.

BAT SPEEDORZ
For venturing to the very back of the Outland's darkest caves, Bats use their Speedorz. Blista's Bat Speedor has Bat wing extensions to provide extra lift when jumping obstacles.

Gormless grin

Pink nose distinguishes Blista from Braptor.

Glowing CHI trident

DISTRACTION TECHNIQUE
Considering the size of the Bat army, to call Blista their best warrior is quite an accolade. However, he is so easily distracted that even though he's a strong and fast fighter, his enemies can usually outsmart him.

CHIMA FILE

LIKES Practical jokes

DISLIKES
Landing on his head

BEST PAL Braptor

ARCHENEMIES
Chima tribes

Bat symbol on belt

115

SCORM
SCORPION MEGALOMANIAC

Insane King of the Scorpions, Scorm wants to rule all of Chima, now! He is obsessed with stealing all CHI in his bid for world domination. The leaders of the other Outland Tribes go along with his plans—it's less dangerous than disagreeing.

Top of skull emblazened with Scorpion.

STING IN THE TAIL
Like most Scorpions, Scorm can control other people's minds using a special toxin in his tail, but not for long. Unfortunately the effect wears off after a few moments.

Did you know?
Scorm believes in "The Great Scorpion in the Sky:" a mythical being who dropped CHI so that the Scorpions could evolve.

Powerful toxic tail

EVIL BOSS
You can learn a lot about an individual by how they treat their underlings, and Scorm abuses Scolder and Scutter constantly. When things don't go his way, he takes it out on them, smacking them round the head with his barbed tail.

Golden kingly armor

CHIMA FILE

LIKES Power

DISLIKES His orders not being obeyed

BEST PAL Queen Spinlyn

ARCHENEMIES Anyone who threatens his position

SCOLDER
SECOND-IN-COMMAND

Scolder is an unusual specimen within the Scorpion Tribe, in that he actually has some smarts. That doesn't mean that he gets any less abuse from King Scorm—in fact, he is constantly being sharply put back in his place!

BRAINS TO BOOT
The long-suffering Scolder patiently puts up with King Scorm's ridiculing. Fortunately, Scolder is so intelligent that he can often outsmart his rivals. Along with his sharp fighting instinct, this makes him the complete soldiering package.

ARMED FOR ATTACK
Scolder rides his special Scorpion Speedor into battle. It comes equipped with upgraded attack extensions resembling a Scorpion's tail and pincers.

Sinister yellow eyes

Sharp fangs

Silver markings display lower ranking than King Scorm

Green coloring of Outland Tribe

◎ CHIMA FILE

LIKES *Thinking his way through problems*

DISLIKES *Being hit by Scorm*

BEST PAL *Scutter*

ARCHENEMY *Scorm, but don't tell anyone*

Did you know?
Scolder secretly yearns for power. He's just waiting for Scorm to finally lose his mind so he can step into the breach.

SCUTTER
STAMPING STOMPER

Brutish Scutter is a Scorpion Stomper—a Scorpion soldier who walks on six large legs. Stompers are immensely strong and powerful, but do not possess much in the way of brains. When King Scorm issues a threat, Scutter is the one to carry it out.

TAKING ORDERS
Scutter doesn't have the intelligence to think for himself, so he's happy to take orders from Scorm. Mostly, Scutter just lets his size and strength do the talking (and thinking!).

Toxic tail

Sharp spear filled with Scorpion poison

Deadly fangs

Serious all-black uniform

Six legs of a Scorpion Stomper

 CHIMA FILE

LIKES Attacking enemies

DISLIKES Losing battles

BEST PAL Scorm

ARCHENEMY Scolder

LETHAL WEAPON
Most Scorpions only have the power to sting with their tails when in close combat. Stompers, however, have tails that can blast toxic liquid over long distances. Watch out!

SPINLYN

VAIN SPIDER QUEEN

Spider queen Spinlyn is more concerned with preening than ruling. While the other Outland leaders want CHI to become more powerful, Spinlyn believes that it will make her more beautiful. To her, beauty is power, and she wields it like a weapon.

IN THE EYE OF THE BEHOLDER
Giant fangs and a black-and-gold ridged head might not be everyone's idea of beauty, but to the Spider Tribe, Spinlyn is akin to a goddess. To anyone not a Spider, she looks revolting!

BEAUTY ARMOR
Spinlyn is so vain that she would never go into battle without full makeup and perfect hair. It's more important to her than weapons or armor! However, as backup, she wields her long legs like swords in a fight.

Sleek gold highlights

Webstafa weapon with poisonous spikes

Bulbous body of a Spider queen

Did you know?
Spinlyn is always worrying about her appearance. Once she captured Plovar the tooth-picking bird so that he could tidy her fangs with his beak!

Spindly legs for multitasking or skewering enemies

◎ CHIMA FILE

LIKES Mirrors

DISLIKES Bad fang days!

BEST PALS Her adoring Spider minions

ARCHENEMIES Chima's "heroes"

SPARACON
CHIEF SPIDER SOLDIER

Chief Spider soldier Sparacon is cold and calculating. You can never quite be sure what's going on behind those eight eyes of his. He is clever and inventive, and never shows any warmth or friendliness.

MASTERMIND
Sparacon brings brains and creativity to the Spider Tribe. He helped to design many of their weapons—including his favorite, the Carapace blaster, named and shaped to look like a Spider's very own exoskeleton.

Cold, calculating, yellow eyes

Sinister skulls adorn kneepads.

Did you know?
Spider soldiers use their "Spider Steel" webs for building traps and cages and even blocking Mount Cavora's waterfalls.

TWO, FOUR, SIX, EIGHT
As a Spider soldier, Sparacon has four legs that can be used for spinning and shooting webs. He uses his two spare arms to fight with his blaster, and his other two legs for staying upright. Some multitasking!

Sharpened fangs at the ready.

Tangled spider web sticks CHI to chest.

 CHIMA FILE

LIKES Keeping a cool head

DISLIKES Showing emotions

BEST PAL
Friends are for wimps

ARCHENEMY
Potentially everyone

SPARRATUS
LOYAL SPIDER DRONE

Being a four-legged Spider drone, Sparratus is as evolved as he will ever be. No matter how much this tough Spider practices his web-building, he will never match the skills of the eight-legged soldiers he aspires to be.

ASSAULT VEHICLE
Sparratus's souped-up armored vehicle has a CHI-powered engine, all-terrain tires, spider detailing, and deadly accurate missiles. Just the job for an assault on the Chima Tribes.

THE JOKER
Ambitious Sparratus dutifully follows orders, but still makes time to have fun and play jokes on the prisoners he guards. There's nothing he enjoys more than spinning a funny beard or hairdo out of web, and dressing up his hapless victims!

Four limbs are a source of frustration—Sparratus longs for eight.

Hapless lines of misspun web drape body.

Eight spider eyes give wide range of vision.

Brown exoskeleton

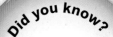

⊚ CHIMA FILE

LIKES Playing jokes

DISLIKES Not being a Spider soldier

BEST PAL Sparacon

ARCHENEMY Anyone who threatens Queen Spinlyn

Did you know?
So desperate to be a Spider soldier, Sparratus once stuck fake legs to his back. Sadly, they kept falling off.

SCORM'S SCORPION STINGER

ASSAULT VEHICLE

This stinging assault vehicle attacks with massive pincing claws and shoots toxic venomballs from its tail. If you're unlucky enough to get too close, there are poisonous fangs to be wary of too!

BRUTE POWER

The Scorpion Stinger is Scorm's pride and joy. Just like the Scorpion Tribe, the Stinger is powerful and aggressive, and shows no mercy to the opposition. Scorm finds it more trustworthy than the Scorpions in his army.

Toxic venomball

Gleaming red "eyes"

Poison fangs work like daggers.

Deadly grasping pincers

CHIMA FILE

HOME TRIBE Scorpions

CARRIES One Scorpion

SECRET WEAPON Venomballs

PERFECT FOR All out attack!

Did you know?
Scorm needs to keep an eye behind him when driving the Stinger—the rear is the only unprotected area, and vulnerable to attack.

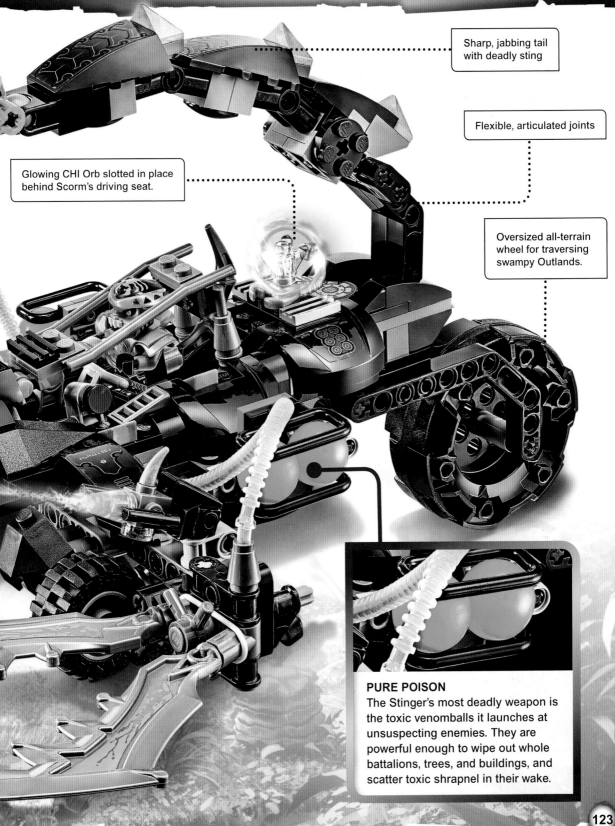

Sharp, jabbing tail with deadly sting

Flexible, articulated joints

Glowing CHI Orb slotted in place behind Scorm's driving seat.

Oversized all-terrain wheel for traversing swampy Outlands.

PURE POISON
The Stinger's most deadly weapon is the toxic venomballs it launches at unsuspecting enemies. They are powerful enough to wipe out whole battalions, trees, and buildings, and scatter toxic shrapnel in their wake.

LAVERTUS'S OUTLANDS BASE
OUTLAW'S SECRET HOME

Exiled from Chima, Lavertus made a home for himself in the Outlands. Over the years, his lair has evolved to resemble a miniature Lion City, but with local influences of crawling weeds and vines. Superbly camouflaged, it is protected by multiple weapons—and the occasional carniverous plant!

◎ CHIMA FILE

HOME TRIBE None

LOCATION Secret location deep in the Outlands

SECRET WEAPON Hand-cranked machine gun

PERFECT FOR Hiding out

JUNGLE WORKSHOP

Lavertus is a genius when it comes to inventing and creating weapons, vehicles, and technology. His jungle base is the perfect place to work on his new inventions—such as his new two-wheeled Lion Bike—in peace.

Spider webs adorn the walls

Machine gun blasts multiple shots at once, fueled by CHI energy.

Crank for winding gun

Bold yellow coloring of the Lion Tribe.

Did you know?
Lavertus's lair can only be accessed through an obstacle-filled route that is highly reminiscent of a Speedor track.

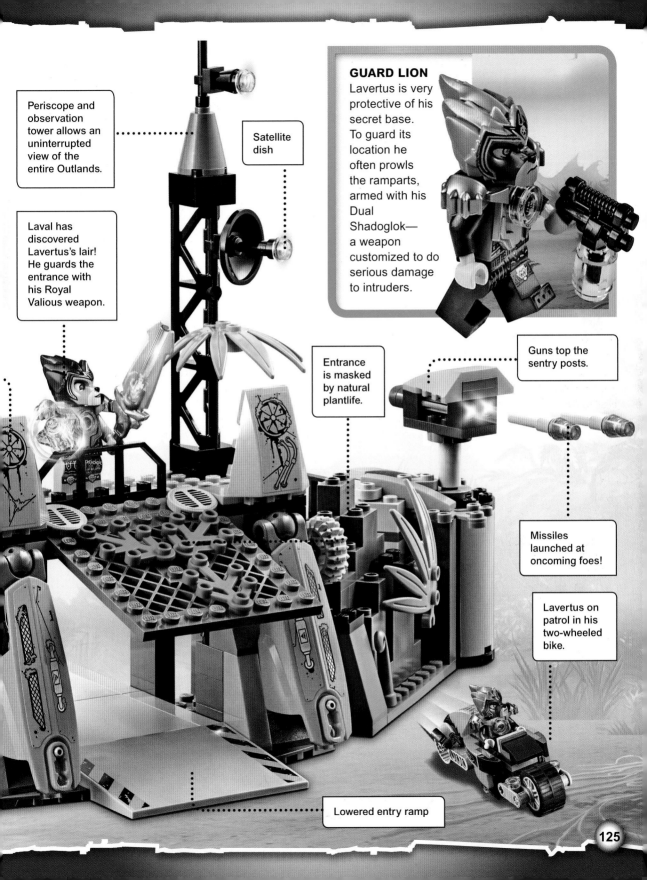

Periscope and observation tower allows an uninterrupted view of the entire Outlands.

Satellite dish

GUARD LION
Lavertus is very protective of his secret base. To guard its location he often prowls the ramparts, armed with his Dual Shadoglok—a weapon customized to do serious damage to intruders.

Laval has discovered Lavertus's lair! He guards the entrance with his Royal Valious weapon.

Entrance is masked by natural plantlife.

Guns top the sentry posts.

Missiles launched at oncoming foes!

Lavertus on patrol in his two-wheeled bike.

Lowered entry ramp

SPINLYN'S SPIDER CAVERN
DEADLY LAIR

Deep in the darkest corner of the Outlands, the evil Spider queen Spinlyn has made her home. Full of deadly traps and webs, the creepy Spider Cavern is an inhospitable hovel for anyone other than a shadows-loving Spider. Any heroes who dare to venture here should beware!

◎ CHIMA FILE

HOME TRIBE Spiders

LOCATION The farthest edge of the Outlands

SECRET WEAPON Poisonous fangs

PERFECT FOR Trapping unsuspecting interlopers

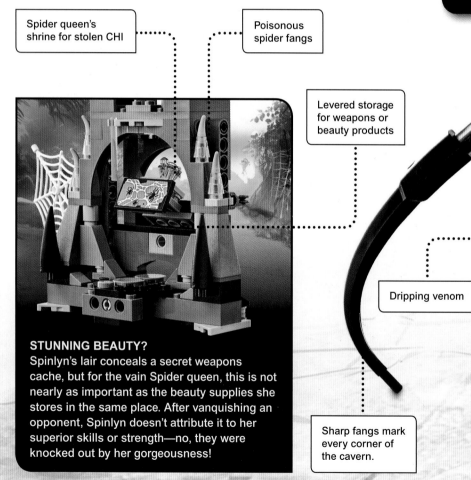

Spider queen's shrine for stolen CHI

Poisonous spider fangs

Spider minion

Levered storage for weapons or beauty products

Dripping venom

STUNNING BEAUTY?
Spinlyn's lair conceals a secret weapons cache, but for the vain Spider queen, this is not nearly as important as the beauty supplies she stores in the same place. After vanquishing an opponent, Spinlyn doesn't attribute it to her superior skills or strength—no, they were knocked out by her gorgeousness!

Sharp fangs mark every corner of the cavern.

Mirror so Spinlyn can admire her reflection.

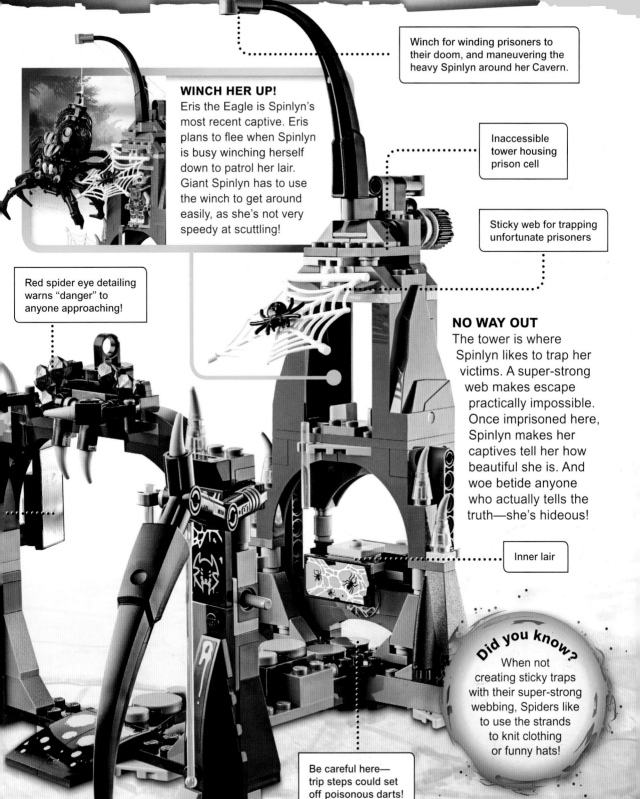

Winch for winding prisoners to their doom, and maneuvering the heavy Spinlyn around her Cavern.

WINCH HER UP!
Eris the Eagle is Spinlyn's most recent captive. Eris plans to flee when Spinlyn is busy winching herself down to patrol her lair. Giant Spinlyn has to use the winch to get around easily, as she's not very speedy at scuttling!

Inaccessible tower housing prison cell

Sticky web for trapping unfortunate prisoners

Red spider eye detailing warns "danger" to anyone approaching!

NO WAY OUT
The tower is where Spinlyn likes to trap her victims. A super-strong web makes escape practically impossible. Once imprisoned here, Spinlyn makes her captives tell her how beautiful she is. And woe betide anyone who actually tells the truth—she's hideous!

Inner lair

Did you know?
When not creating sticky traps with their super-strong webbing, Spiders like to use the strands to knit clothing or funny hats!

Be careful here— trip steps could set off poisonous darts!

SPARRATUS'S SPIDER STALKER
EIGHT-LEGGED HORROR

A huge Spider-shaped assault vehicle, the Spider Stalker walks on eight humongous articulated legs. Its weapons include web missiles, which shoot out fully formed webs—for terrifying arachnophobes Chima-wide!

TWO SPIDERS IN ONE
Lead Spider drone Sparratus commands the Spider Stalker. He is tough and ruthless when behind the controls of his machine, and will trample over anyone in his way.

Vials of poison sit at top of legs.

Weapons cache

Sharp stomping legs

Poison-laden fangs

A STICKY MESS
Like the Spiders themselves, the Stalker is capable of shooting out ready-formed webs to capture and entangle enemies. The sticky webbing is emitted as a massive pipeline-sized stream.

Web shoots out from open jaw.

Strong body can withstand heavy blows.

 CHIMA FILE

HOMETRIBE Spider

CARRIES One Spider

SECRET WEAPON
Poisoned pincers

PERFECT FOR Stomping all over the enemy

OUTLAND WEAPONS
BATTY BLASTERS

Did you know?
The Outland Tribes' weapons have the added factor of being loaded with poisonous liquids to use against their foes.

BAT WEAPONS

Sonorr Blaster

SCORPION WEAPONS

The foot soldiers of the Scorpion army have simple spears and staffs to fight their opponents. However, a Scorpion's best weapon is its tail sting as it's more accurate and more deadly.

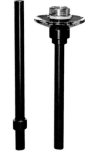

Korrodor

The weakest and dumbest of all the Outland Tribes, the Bats use simple weapons like knives and spears. The most complicated weapons they own are pulse beam blasters.

SPIDER WEAPONS

CHI Stafa　**Clubak**

Stike　**Screptar**

KING SCORM'S KORRODOR

Scorm's powerful venom-shooting blaster has golden fang detailing and a tank full of poison to use on enemies.

Spiara

Pronged Sonoranti

Spikorr

Webstafa

The Spiders are the most intelligent of the Outland Tribes, and their weapons reflect this. Sparacon's giant Blaster is filled with venom and the Spider drones fight with the Weborax, Carapace, or Webstafa.

Carapace Blaster

THE FIRE TRIBES

The wise, immortal Phoenix and the fiercely protective Felines—Tigers, Leopards, and Li'Ella the Lioness—make up the Fire Tribes. United against the malicious Hunter Tribes, these solitary creatures leave their secret home on top of Mount Cavora and join forces with Chima's heroes to fight for their land. Teamwork, combined with the new power of Fire CHI, is the only chance they've got to save their homeland.

Phoenix leader Fluminox drives a fiery Speedor with flaming wings.

FLUMINOX
HIGH-MINDED LEADER

🔥 **CHIMA FILE**

LIKES Study and meditation

DISLIKES Seeing Flinx waste his potential

BEST PAL Tormak

ARCHENEMY Hunters

In the lofty Phoenix City, Fluminox rules his tribe with great wisdom. But his studious mind and serious ways sometimes keep him from understanding how others think and feel. Luckily, he has trusted advisors and years of experience to rely on.

Elaborate crown marks Fluminox as a ruler.

Wide wings have the flame of a mature Phoenix.

Long robes suit a serious, studious lifestyle.

Ancient Phoenix symbols and medallions hang from Fluminox's chain belt.

PHOENIX FORCE
On the ground, calm Fluminox is a surprisingly skillful and powerful fighter who can knock down enemies seemingly effortlessly. And he can create some pretty nifty moves in a Speedor too.

LAUGH-FREE ZONE
Fluminox has a deep knowledge of Chima's ancient history, as well as great patience, logic, and restraint. However, this serious brainbox has no sense of humor—it once took him more than 3000 years to get a joke! And even then he didn't break his composure with a chuckle.

FLINX

FEARLESS YOUNG BIRD

Flinx may be thousands of years old, but in the ancient Phoenix Tribe he's still considered a kid. And he'd rather have fun than worry about big issues like Hunter Tribes and the fate of Chima. After all, his father, Fluminox, is serious enough for the both of them!

BIRD BOMBER
Young Flinx may lack adult wings, but he doesn't lack courage. He is one of three Phoenix pilots trusted to fly the Phoenix Temple, firing fireballs at the enemy at the same time!

Golden detailing to headpiece signifies a future ruler.

Small wings have not yet developed their flame.

Did you know?
Flinx is a rarity in the Phoenix Tribe in not wanting to grow up—all his peers have already developed their flame wings.

Large breastplate holds Fire CHI.

FLEDGLING
Small-statured Flinx is in no hurry to grow up. He's heard plenty of lectures from his dad about how important it is for him to focus on his studies and thus earn his wings like the rest of the tribe, but Flinx reckons he's got plenty of time to worry about that. This little guy is content just the way he is.

🔥 CHIMA FILE

LIKES *Just hanging out*

DISLIKES *Anything too serious*

BEST PAL *Fluminox*

ARCHENEMIES *Hunters*

FIROX
FUN-LOVING GUNNER

Flying goggles help Firox to focus when aiming the Blazing Bastion's guns.

Firox is glad to be a co-pilot and gunner onboard the Blazing Bastion, because the high gun turrets are the best place to be a part of the action! But, if he had his way, Firox would spend all day every day zooming around Cavora with his best friend Frax!

Golden breastplate holds Fire CHI in place.

FAITHFUL FRIEND
Daring Firox and cheeky Frax are brothers-in-arms and can always be found standing side-by-side in battle situations. They share a love of flying the Blazing Bastion, and also for performing wild new stunts. Once they even bungee jumped off the top of Mount Cavora!

Bright red and orange colors of the Phoenix Tribe

Straps fasten Firox in position even on the wildest of flights!

🔥 CHIMA FILE

LIKES Being in the action

DISLIKES Dull moments

BEST PAL Frax

ARCHENEMIES Hunters

FRAX
STUNT GUY

If you can't find Frax in his gun turret, try looking for the nearest towering cliff, slippery slope, or terrifying cave. This thrill-seeking bird is sure to be trying out a crazy new stunt, or acting on a dare from a fellow Phoenix!

Laser-focused eyes are skilled at aiming the Bastion's guns.

Battle-ready expression looks serious, but most of the time Frax is ready for fun!

BASTION CO-PILOT
As a co-pilot and gunner of the Flying Phoenix Fire Temple—the Blazing Bastion—Frax gets a front-row seat to all the action and plays a key role in keeping the Phoenix Tribe safe. It's an important job—but this feathered fun-lover would rather be off having thrilling adventures!

SINGLE SEATER
In this swift one-seated flyer, Frax is more nimble than the Blazing Bastion allows. He can zip in and out of skirmishes during a battle—or just race around Mount Cavora for fun!

FOLTRAX
HOTSHOT PILOT

🔥 **CHIMA FILE**

LIKES Stunts, flying

DISLIKES Being grounded

BEST PALS Fluminox, Frax

ARCHENEMIES Hunters

No one flies the Phoenix Temple quite like fearless Foltrax! His daring maneuvers and aerial stunts call for extreme skill and daring. For his passengers, it can be a wild ride, but they have confidence that this experienced pilot will always get them there safely in the end.

Wide wings glow with flames when in flight.

Intense eyes stay completely focused during flight.

ADRENALINE JUNKIE
When Foltrax flies, the journey is sure to include spins, flips, and daredevil maneuvers! He gets a thrill out of pushing boundaries and having a blast in the pilot seat.

HOT-HEADED
Foltrax loves nothing more than flying high and showing off his moves in the air. After more than 1000 years grounded in the hidden Phoenix City, he can't wait to get behind the controls of a plane again and see the world!

Metallic flight gear wraps around legs and waist.

TORMAK
TRUSTED ADVISOR

Long ago, Tormak the Tiger pledged the Tigers' loyalty to the Phoenix Tribe, and Tormak became Fluminox's most trusted advisor and friend. Tormak is at the heart of all the Phoenix's major decisions. The Phoenix also rely on him to translate Fluminox's puzzling way of speaking!

GREAT DEFENDER
Tormak has been trusted with all the Phoenix's secrets. In return, he is prepared to defend his adoptive family with his life. When the Hunter Tribes attack, he is the very first to race to protect the Phoenix Temple walls.

Did you know?
Tormak and the Tiger Tribe are under the powerful protection of the Phoenix—and are immortal while this protection lasts.

Tough scowl shows Tormak's fierce loyalty to his adopted tribe.

Red-and-gold garments are a mark of acceptance by the Phoenix Tribe.

Strong gold armor protects Tormak in battle.

PROTECTIVE DAD
Tormak's greatest love is his adopted daughter, Li'Ella. He and Fluminox often talk about how challenging their children can be, but when Li'Ella is in trouble, no one could display fiercer loyalty than this tough Tiger—who would fight to the bitter end to protect her.

⊛ CHIMA FILE

LIKES *Knowing all the Phoenix Tribe's secrets*

DISLIKES *Seeing Li'Ella in trouble*

BEST PAL *Fluminox*

ARCHENEMIES *Hunters*

LUNDOR
LOYAL LEOPARD

You can count on Lundor to recall every strike and maneuver of every battle, down to the tiniest detail. His picture-perfect memory captures it all—useful for the guard commanders, but embarrassing for anyone who makes a mistake in battle!

🔥 CHIMA FILE

LIKES Being unique

DISLIKES Disorganization in battle

BEST PALS Members of the Phoenix and Feline Tribes

ARCHENEMIES Hunters

WELL SPOTTED
As a Leopard, Lundor is a close relative of the Tiger Tribe, and he lives alongside them under the protection of the Phoenix. But it is easy to see what sets him apart: He is the only spotted cat among the stripy Tigers.

Leopard's spots are unique to Lundor.

Long-handled Blazeprowlor for staying as far away as possible from Hunter Tribes in battle.

Red uniform shows allegiance to the Tigers and the Phoenix.

Did you know?
Lundor once tried to cover up his spots in order to blend in... but he missed them too much when they were gone!

FIRE BLAST
When the icy Vultures attack, faithful guard Lundor defends the Phoenix Tribe and his friends with all the firepower he can find.

LI'ELLA
LIONESS LIEUTENANT

Tough Li'Ella is top lieutenant to her adoptive Tiger father, Tormak. For thousands of years she lived among the Phoenix and Tigers, believing she was the only one of her kind— until she met Laval and discovered she's not the only Lion in Chima after all!

GIRL GUARD
It's Li'Ella's job to help protect her adoptive tribe as a Guard— and she's one of the best. Smart, strong, and skilled, she's an expert at handling weapons of all kinds.

Maneless head is unique to Li'Ella—the only known Lioness in Chima.

Large golden breastplate hides a decorative top underneath.

Wrap skirt covers the tops of Li'Ella's legs.

SELF-SUFFICIENT
To Tormak, Li'Ella is the little daughter he'll always want to protect. But if there's anyone who doesn't need protection, it's Li'Ella! She can hold her own in a battle against the Hunters and can disarm with charm, too: Laval is practically speechless when he meets this pretty Lioness!

🔥 CHIMA FILE

LIKES Defending the tribe

DISLIKES Being treated like a little girl

BEST PAL Tormak, and maybe Laval if she gives him a chance

ARCHENEMIES Hunters

FLYING PHOENIX
FIRE TEMPLE
BLAZING BASTION

At Mount Cavora's uppermost peak hides this flame-red temple, designed to leave visitors awestruck. It's the perfect place for Fluminox's high-level meetings, tribal ceremonies, or just quiet contemplation. When it's time for action, the entire top of the temple lifts off to become an amazing flying fighting machine.

Powerful fireball blaster controlled by a swinging catapult mechanism.

Fireballs inflict maximum damage on enemies.

Emblazoned Phoenix symbol

Fireballs released through the base of the flying temple.

LIFT OFF! With a few dramatic alterations, the top of the Temple becomes a flying machine called the Blazing Bastion! Trust the daring trio of Foltrax, Firox, and Frax to pilot the Bastion through any obstacle!

Temple walls fold back to become wings for flying.

HOME TRIBE *Phoenix*

LOCATION *Top of Mount Cavora*

SECRET WEAPON *Detachable flying ship*

PERFECT FOR *A remote base for the Phoenix Tribe*

Did you know?
King Fluminox has a severe aversion to flying. When the Fire Temple is in flight mode he sits well back and away from the controls.

Phoenix-head shaped temple roof becomes a cockpit.

CHIMA'S BEST KEPT SECRET

A powerful and magical energy concealed the Fire Temple at the top of Mount Cavora. But when the waterfalls were frozen by the newly awakened Hunter Tribes, the Phoenix elders sent Eris a vision revealing their location so that they could come together to fight off the new threat to their land.

Torch holders become talons in flight.

Gated entrance on Mount Cavora admits only a select, trusted few.

FIRE TRIBES' WEAPONS
FLAMING FIRE POWER

What is the main goal of a Fire Tribe weapon? To blast through icy defenses and melt, melt, melt! These swords, spears, and blasters add a fiery blaze to every strike, melting through walls of ice and disarming the enemy with a combination of force and heat.

TORMAK'S TYGAFYRE
As head of the Phoenix Guard, it's only fitting that Tormak should get to use this fiery phenomenon. With four Orbs of Fire CHI, it's definitely one of the hottest things in Chima!

Fire CHI slotted into position.

Extra-large frame acts as a shield as well as a weapon.

Tormak growls menacingly as he heads into battle!

Red-hot flames burst from the side—but won't singe Tormak.

Fiery pulse beams shoot from the front of the Tygafyre.

SMALL BUT MIGHTY

These basic spikes, ax, and whip might seem simple—if they were used by anyone other than the red-hot Fire Tribe! Fire CHI adds searing heat to a strike by the spikes or ax. As for the whip—its lightning-fast speed gives it all the heat it needs.

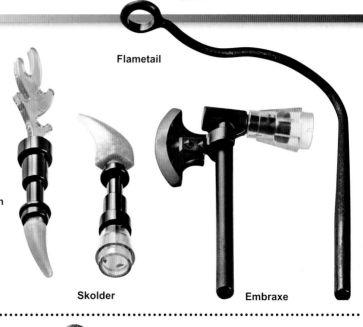

Flametail

Fyretalon

Skolder

Embraxe

Li'Ella's Roarburn

SUPER STAFFS

Long handles and dangerous tips make these staffs perfect for fighting on foot or from a vehicle. With extra-long reach, they're perfect for stopping an icy blast from a safe distance!

ADVANCED WEAPONRY

Lundor's Blazeprowlor

BEST OF BOTH WORLDS

With golden handles at the bottom and razor-thin blades at the top, these well-crafted weapons represent the best of the Fire Tribe: the perfect balance between land, sky, and fighting power!

Phoenix Emberstaf

FLIGHT READY

For the Phoenix and other airborne fighters, aerodynamics are key, and every detail matters! The handles of these two Phoenix blades are short and light, and balanced with a counterweight at the bottom.

Flinx's Flikker

FIRE SUITS

GIFTS FROM THE PHOENIX

In order to help in the fight against the Hunters, the Phoenix give a select few heroes from Chima new armor and weapons to match. This brave gang are now protected by the Phoenix's powers, and can wield Fire CHI without any risk of damage to themselves.

Did you know?
Fire CHI is extremely precious and, as such, only given to those deemed worthy or capable of using it.

GORZAN

With the extraordinary power of Fire CHI, Gorzan's new armored tank becomes a fire-breathing attack vehicle. With hefty armor plating designed to look like an angry Gorilla, this beast rolls across the ice on wheels with tires specially designed for Chima's new wintry conditions.

Gorzan wears his new Fire suit.

Burner Basha

Blazing fire blaster

Fiery Phoenix symbol

FIRED UP!

RAZAR

Chief Raven thief Razar is super impressed with his new suit and Insinasabre sword—they might fetch a nice price on the black market after the fighting is over!

LAGRAVIS

King LaGravis is more determined than anyone to restore peace to Chima. His Royal Valious is now equipped with Fire CHI power.

LAVAL

When it's close to Fire CHI, Laval's Speedor grows claws made of fire! Now he can race after the Hunters, armed with his sharp Skolder sword.

ERIS

Eris has a special connection with the Phoenix Tribe and dreams about bursting into flames. Will she ever want to take off her Fire suit and return to the Eagle Tribe?

CRAGGER

Reunited with best friend Laval, Cragger is eager to join the others and defeat the Hunters. His new gear is fierce enough to confront these new foes.

WORRIZ

Who knows whether Worriz can really be trusted? However, he has proven himself to be an excellent fighter with this new Howlthrowa weapon.

THE HUNTER TRIBES

After several millennia of frozen sleep, the Hunter Tribes have awoken and emerged from underground. Thousands of years in the ice have given the vicious Saber-tooth Tigers, the Mammoths, and the Vultures the ability to control ice and freeze the land and other tribes. Now the Hunters want to finish what they started many years ago—to rule all of Chima and keep all the CHI for themselves.

Maula's Ice Mammoth Stomper marches formidably across the ice!

147

SIR FANGAR
VENGEFUL DICTATOR

Deranged leader of the Saber-tooth Tigers, "Sir" Fangar sees himself as a cultured and philosophical soul. Intent on taking over the world, he likes to think of himself as an artist and benefactor whose reign will enlighten the inhabitants of Chima.

Winter cape—good for looking important, as well as keeping warm!

THE GREAT COLLECTOR
Sir Fangar likes to collect and freeze his prisoners and store them in his Ice Palace as museum pieces. He has even been known to talk to them, although their frozen state means they cannot reply. His greatest, unfulfilled, desire is to capture a Phoenix—one of the rarest creatures in all of Chima.

Body was once completely covered with snowy white fur.

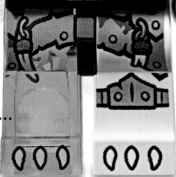

ADVANCING ARMY
If the bold Sir Fangar has one fault, it's that he never knows when to retreat. Vehicles like this heavy-duty tank mean his army doesn't often need to!

Whole leg entirely consumed by ice.

148

STEALTHOR
GENERAL-IN-CHIEF

Trusted with the Hunters' armies, Stealthor is a ruthless and commanding leader. He leads from the front, going ahead to scout for the unsuspecting tribes of Chima. If you spot Stealthor, you can be sure that hordes of fierce soldiers are not far behind.

SWIFT AND SILENT
Stealthor's stealthy three-wheeled trike is both fast and silent. This makes it the perfect vehicle for scouting for the enemy in icy Chima—where any sound would travel for miles.

GLOW BONES

In the good old days, Stealthor was a master of camouflage. He blended into his surroundings and was super hard to spot. But now, after thousands of years spent decaying in the ice, his exposed bones glow brightly whenever he uses CHI. Not great for sneaking up on people in the dark!

Narrowed eyes scour the landscape far and wide.

⊛ CHIMA FILE

LIKES Getting up to no good

DISLIKES Being caught red-handed

BEST PAL Sir Fangar

ARCHEMENIES Phoenix

After years spent underground, Stealthor's body has aged, and now patches of flesh show through his fur.

Fierce weapon adds extra-sharp claw power.

STRAINOR
NERVOUS LIEUTENANT

Paranoid Saber-tooth Tiger Strainor has been given a raw deal in life so far. Since he was put in charge of Sykor, life has been one long rollercoaster of pain. Sykor is always hurting his nervous keeper—leaving Strainor constantly on edge!

✷ **CHIMA FILE**

LIKES Being far away from Sykor

DISLIKES His job, babysitting Sykor

BEST PAL Stealthor

ARCHENEMY Sykor!

Scars inflicted by Sykor

Sword with razor-sharp edges.

ATTACK VEHICLE
Strainor's ClawRider launches from the top of the Ice Fortress and is often at the forefront of the Saber-tooth Tigers' advance. With double spears at the front, Strainor's ClawRider strikes fear into the hearts of those it faces down.

AVOIDANCE TACTICS
In the heat of battle, Strainor can hold his own. But it's not because he's fighting to win, it's because he wants to avoid more pain! Frankly, Strainor has had enough of being the victim of violence, so he goes all out in order to avoid receiving any further injuries.

Exposed muscle and bone

SYKOR
MANIACAL FIGHTER

All Saber-tooth Tigers are aggressive and violent, but most have learnt to control their impulses. Not Sykor. Totally out of control, Sykor charges around with no restraint, and is just as likely to attack his own tribe as the enemy.

SPEEDY SYKOR
On the rare occasion that Sykor is given free rein, he speeds across the ice on his customized Ice Cruiser, safe in the knowledge that this vehicle has all sorts of mean weapons attached. Sykor loves to feel the wind in his fur as he races along!

✦ CHIMA FILE

LIKES Violence

DISLIKES Peace and quiet

BEST PAL Sykor has no place for emotions, especially not friendly ones

ARCHEMENY Anything that moves!

SLEEPING TIGERS
No-one knows how or why Skykor became as crazed as he is. One thing's for sure, if the Hunter Tribes ever need a break from this beserk warrior, they could just confiscate his CHI—then he'd fall straight back into a deep, frozen sleep.

Padlock ensures Sykor can be locked up and can't run away!

Chains usually held by Strainor

Did you know?
Sykor hasn't learnt how to talk—he just growls at everyone and everything. There's no need for words when you're this fierce!

Clothes ripped in a fight, or when bored and left to his own devices.

MAULA
MOTHER MAMMOTH

As head of the Mammoth Tribe, Maula is a demanding leader—always bossing her non-identical twin sons around. Maula is both overly protective and interfering when it comes to her two children, but while she dotes on Mungus, she barely notices poor neglected Mottrot.

⊛ CHIMA FILE

LIKES *Being in charge, smothering her sons*

DISLIKES *Threats to her children, Mottrot demanding attention*

BEST PAL *Mungus*

ARCHENEMIES *Phoenix*

Kindly eyes belie fierce temper.

Rotting flesh on trunk

Vicious tusks

BRUTE FORCE
Maula always has her sons' backs. In battle, she relies on her Mamzooka blaster to protect them. The cannon shoots icy blasts that freeze their targets on impact.

Matted fur wraps around tops of legs.

FAMILY UNIT
Maula and her sons are among the Hunters' fiercest fighters. With Mottrot's brains and Mungus's strength, they are a force to be reckoned with. And if anyone threatens Maula's prized "baby," Mungus, she sees red and attacks with stunning ferocity.

MOTTROT
RUNT OF THE PACK

Constantly overshadowed by his brother, Mungus, Mottrot is often ignored by the Hunter Tribes—even though he is one of the most intelligent and insightful creatures around. What he lacks in size and power, he makes up for in accelerated intelligence.

UNFAIR TREATMENT
In the Mammoth Tribe, size and strength are more important than intelligence. But Mottrot doesn't complain—even when his great ideas are unfairly attributed to Mungus. He's too busy seeking attention and affection from his mother.

✪ CHIMA FILE

LIKES *Planning, thinking*

DISLIKES *Being ignored by his mother*

BEST PAL *Maula*

ARCHENEMY *Mungus*

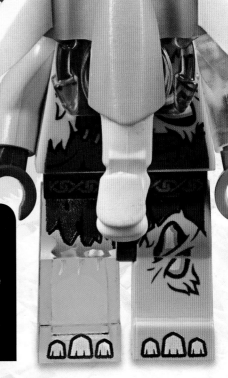

Exposed brain has above average intelligence.

Large ears listen out for inspiration for good ideas.

Armor built from solid ice

OVERSIZED
Mottrot's double-ended spear has two giant tusks. As Mammoth weapons are often built for someone of Mungus's size, this spear is almost too big for Mottrot to handle.

MUNGUS
GIANT SIMPLETON

Mungus's sheer size makes him one of the main warriors of the Hunter Tribes. He seems like a harmless low-intelligence individual, but he's very capable at following orders—when his mother Maula tells him to attack, he does.

Did you know? It takes three whole CHI Orbs to wake up the mighty Mungus from his frozen sleep.

Thick fur provides warmth.

Tung-Tuska club for going into battle against multiple foes.

Three CHI Orbs in belt.

SIBLING RIVALRY
Big, bumbling Mungus can do no wrong in his mother's eyes. Mother Mammoth bestows all her love and attention on her largest son, even praising him for all of his brother Mottrot's good ideas. This makes Mungus very happy—as does beating someone with his club.

✪ CHIMA FILE

LIKES *Fighting*

DISLIKES *Thinking*

BEST PAL *Maula*

ARCHENEMY *Phoenix*

VARDY
VICIOUS VULTURE LEADER

Leading a tribe that is naturally lazy and unambitious is the unenviable task that falls to Vardy. This Vulture leads by example, pursuing his prey for days on end, and earning a reputation for being the cruellest of all the Hunters.

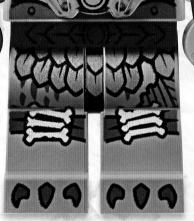

A LITTLE PATIENCE
After setting ice traps to catch unwary victims, Vardy whiles away the time playing crosswords, doing origami, or even whistling. This method of hunting irritates his victims, who would rather face Vardy in a fair fight, than freeze slowly to death.

Huge wingspan

Vulture feather symbols on helmet

✪ CHIMA FILE

LIKES *His evil plans coming to fruition*

DISLIKES *Impatience*

BEST PAL *Himself*

ARCHENEMIES *Phoenix*

Did you know?
Vardy can outwait anyone or anything. He's renowned for saying that he can wait all day for something—or even all year!

VORNON
MISTER NEGATIVE

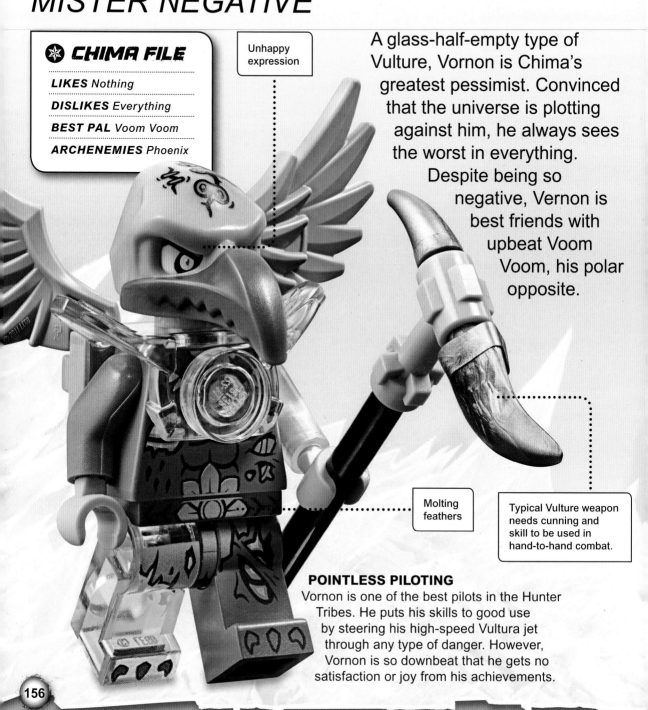

✸ CHIMA FILE

LIKES Nothing

DISLIKES Everything

BEST PAL Voom Voom

ARCHENEMIES Phoenix

Unhappy expression

A glass-half-empty type of Vulture, Vornon is Chima's greatest pessimist. Convinced that the universe is plotting against him, he always sees the worst in everything. Despite being so negative, Vernon is best friends with upbeat Voom Voom, his polar opposite.

Molting feathers

Typical Vulture weapon needs cunning and skill to be used in hand-to-hand combat.

POINTLESS PILOTING
Vornon is one of the best pilots in the Hunter Tribes. He puts his skills to good use by steering his high-speed Vultura jet through any type of danger. However, Vornon is so downbeat that he gets no satisfaction or joy from his achievements.

VOOM VOOM
EVER-EAGER PILOT

Voom Voom is not your typical Vulture. Unlike most of his tribe, who are lazy, calculating, and cold, Voom Voom thinks everything is amazing and fun! With a Vulture's natural piloting skills, this happy and excitable Vulture relishes each and every victory.

A sheepish grin is never far from Voom Voom's expression.

OPPOSITES ATTRACT
Voom Voom is yin to Vornon's yang. Without each other, they'd be lost. Voom Voom's constant optimism—although annoying—actually helps Vornon on his most negative days. Likewise, Vornon's persistent pessimism stops Voom Voom getting carried away on a tidal wave of excitement.

Bone used in attempt to patch up Voom Voom's worse-for-wear body.

ZOOM ZOOM
Taking the power of flight one step further, the Vultures have customized their Speedorz. Elegant wings give these predators greater gliding power.

Moldy green feathers

SIR FANGAR'S
ICE FORTRESS
ICY HOME FROM HOME

The Hunter Tribes live in this sprawling ice fort on a giant glacier, moving slowly but surely toward their goal—the Lion City. This skeletal building has a dark and mysterious history. Recovered from the Gorge of Eternal Depth, and pushed above ground by the Hunter Tribes' ice powers, the fortress is a weapon in itself, turning everything it touches to ice.

Did you know?
Underneath the Ice Fortress lies a labyrinth of caves where Sir Fangar keeps the frozen bodies of his vanquished foes!

TWISTED TOWER
The Ice Fortress owes its crooked appearance and unsound structure to the icy base that it rests upon. The glacier was severely deformed when it was forced up out of the Gorge of Eternal Depth, and the fortress now teeters on the edge, looking as if it might collapse at any moment!

Ice bridge flips to stop trespassers—causing them to fall into the glacier.

Massive fang-like pillars form the base of the Ice Fortress's defence.

HIGH AND MIGHTY
Sir Fangar monitors the progress of his world-takeover plan from an icy throne at the top of his fortress. The glacier and the Ice Fortress move so slowly that most of Chima's animals can march faster than it, but its progress is steady and unstoppable nonetheless.

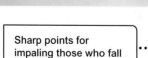

Sharp points for impaling those who fall

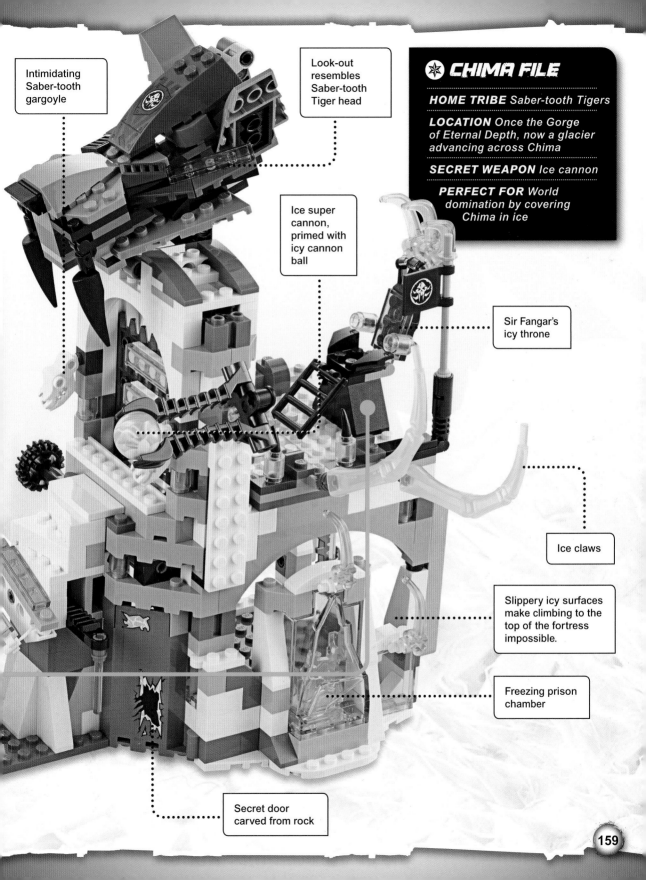

Intimidating
Saber-tooth
gargoyle

Look-out
resembles
Saber-tooth
Tiger head

★ CHIMA FILE

HOME TRIBE Saber-tooth Tigers

LOCATION Once the Gorge
of Eternal Depth, now a glacier
advancing across Chima

SECRET WEAPON Ice cannon

PERFECT FOR World
domination by covering
Chima in ice

Ice super
cannon,
primed with
icy cannon
ball

Sir Fangar's
icy throne

Ice claws

Slippery icy surfaces
make climbing to the
top of the fortress
impossible.

Freezing prison
chamber

Secret door
carved from rock

SIR FANGAR'S
SABER-TOOTH WALKER

AKA THE SABERSTROYER

This four-legged mech is Sir Fangar's pride and joy, and a terror to everyone else! The SaberStroyer is heavily armored as well as brutally armed—perfect for launching all-out attacks on the Chima Tribes. Glowing with the power of blue Ice CHI, the menacing Walker is a fright to behold.

Snapping jaws

FRONT ROW SEAT
Pompous Sir Fangar loves sitting high on top in the cockpit—where he gets the best view of the battlefield below. He can also wallop his enemies with missiles from the twin Ice Pulsorz on each side of his seat. All he needs now is some popcorn!

WALKING ON ICE
Thanks to its massive claws, the hardy Saber-tooth Walker can get a grip on slippery surfaces so climbing up icy mountains is no problem. The bulky vehicle may not be built for speedy chases, but it creates a trail of destruction as it lumbers into battle.

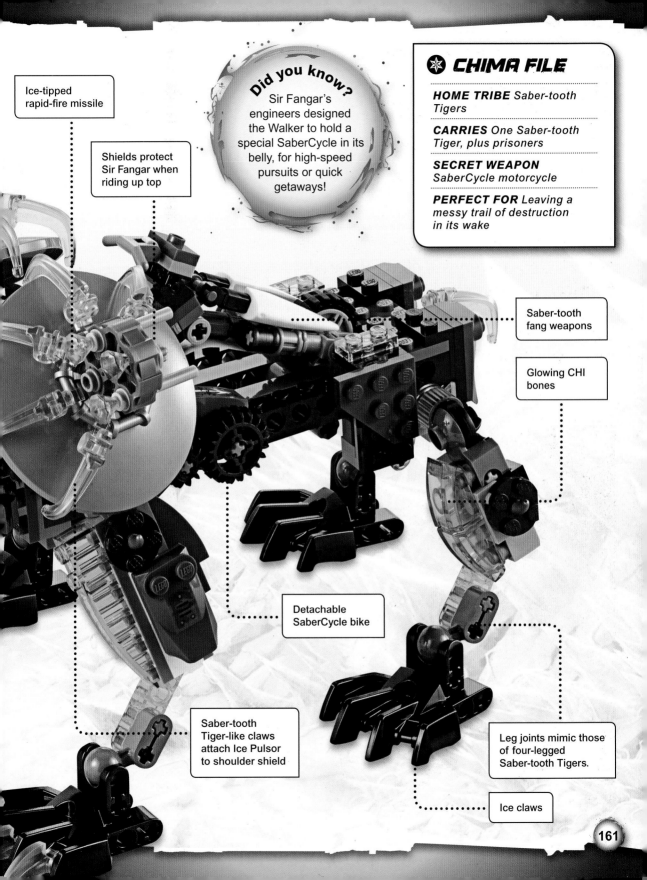

Ice-tipped
rapid-fire missile

Shields protect
Sir Fangar when
riding up top

Did you know?
Sir Fangar's
engineers designed
the Walker to hold a
special SaberCycle in its
belly, for high-speed
pursuits or quick
getaways!

⊛ **CHIMA FILE**

HOME TRIBE Saber-tooth
Tigers

CARRIES One Saber-tooth
Tiger, plus prisoners

SECRET WEAPON
SaberCycle motorcycle

PERFECT FOR Leaving a
messy trail of destruction
in its wake

Saber-tooth
fang weapons

Glowing CHI
bones

Detachable
SaberCycle bike

Saber-tooth
Tiger-like claws
attach Ice Pulsor
to shoulder shield

Leg joints mimic those
of four-legged
Saber-tooth Tigers.

Ice claws

161

MAULA'S ICE MAMMOTH STOMPER

MAMA'S TOY

Any vehicle of Maula's would have to be mammoth in size and scope. Trudging its way across the ice plains on four hulking legs, the Ice Mammoth Stomper is nigh unstoppable, and the largest of the Hunter attack vehicles.

MIGHTY BEAST

In battle, the Ice Stomper blasts opponents with its ice cannon and then, when up close and personal, sideswipes enemies with its ferocious tusks. And if all else fails, the occupants can make a quick getaway on the detachable flyer.

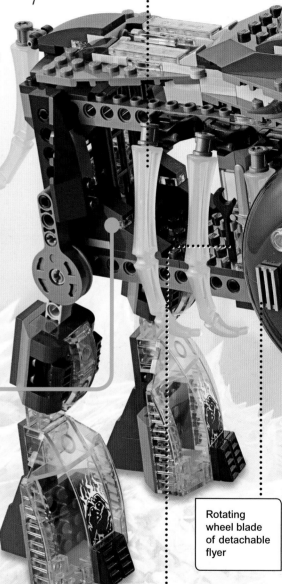

Icy rib bones encase prison cell.

Rotating wheel blade of detachable flyer

Wrench and weapons for emergency situations stored within easy reach.

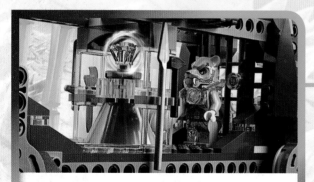

COLD ISOLATION

The "belly" of the Mammoth Stomper is a prison that only the most foolhardy would try and escape from. If an unfortunate captive gets past the icy ribcage bars and the Saber-tooth guard, then there's a long drop to the ground and great clunking feet to dodge.

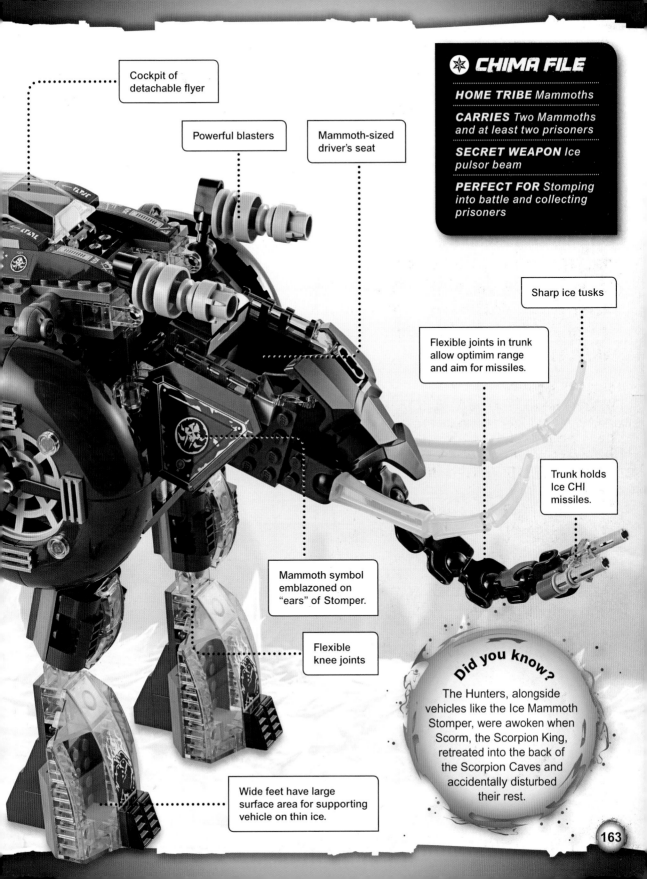

Cockpit of
detachable flyer

Powerful blasters

Mammoth-sized
driver's seat

✳ **CHIMA FILE**

HOME TRIBE Mammoths

CARRIES Two Mammoths
and at least two prisoners

SECRET WEAPON Ice
pulsor beam

PERFECT FOR Stomping
into battle and collecting
prisoners

Sharp ice tusks

Flexible joints in trunk
allow optimim range
and aim for missiles.

Trunk holds
Ice CHI
missiles.

Mammoth symbol
emblazoned on
"ears" of Stomper.

Flexible
knee joints

Did you know?

The Hunters, alongside
vehicles like the Ice Mammoth
Stomper, were awoken when
Scorm, the Scorpion King,
retreated into the back of
the Scorpion Caves and
accidentally disturbed
their rest.

Wide feet have large
surface area for supporting
vehicle on thin ice.

VARDY'S ICE VULTURE GLIDER

SUPER-COOL JET

Built in the Vulture's own image, Vardy's Ice Vulture Glider has feathered wings, a beaked head, and an aerodynamic shape for circling the skies. Its agile and graceful style belies its evil intention—to steal CHI!

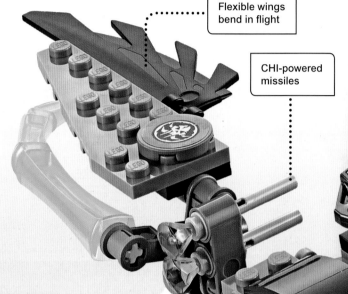

Flexible wings bend in flight

CHI-powered missiles

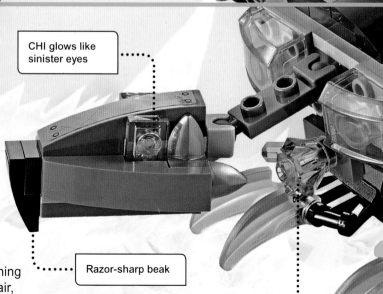

CHI glows like sinister eyes

SCAREDY-VULTURES
For those rare occasions when cowardly Vardy gets cornered, his glider has a detachable cockpit—perfect for a speedy getaway.

COLD AS ICE
Powered by Ice CHI, the Ice Vulture spreads a frozen trail in its wake. Its rapid-fire missiles can transform any target into an icy statue, and any incoming pulse beams are simply frozen in mid-air, dropping harmlessly to the ground.

Razor-sharp beak

CHI Orb in position

Did you know?
This vehicle is Vardy's favorite. He calls it the "Vultura" and is particularly fond of its speed—both into and out of battle.

Steering controls for directing the glider with ease and precision

Detachable cockpit

ATTACK MODE
The Ice Vulture Glider is perfect for circling the skies on the prowl for enemies. However, Vultures leave nothing to chance and also set traps for victims to ensare themselves upon.

Rear thruster

Symbol of the Vulture Tribe

✦ *CHIMA FILE*

HOME TRIBE *Vultures*

CARRIES *One Vulture*

SECRET WEAPON *Detachable flyer*

PERFECT FOR *Surprise attacks and quick getaways*

Icy talons help grasp snow and ice when glider walks on two legs.

Aerodynamic feathered wings

HUNTER TRIBE
WEAPONS
ICY INSTRUMENTS

The Hunter Tribes' weapons are menacing instruments, often with attachments carved from ice itself. Although most are primitive spears and axes that lay unused beneath the ice for millennia, they are no less effective than any other tribes' weapons.

Did you know?
The Hunters' favorite weapon—the Ice Pulsorz—shoot out pulse beams of ice that instantly freeze anything they touch.

Pauldrons top off icy armor.

Double Axicles

CHI Orb

ICY BLADES
Voom Voom's two ice axes have seriously sharp blades, which turn everything they touch to ice! As a "hands-on" type of warrior, Voom Voom would rather be in the midst of the action than shooting from a distance, so he prefers these axes to a Pulsor weapon.

Voom Voom requires both arms to fight with two axes at once.

Blades were made of metal before they froze.

166

SABER-TOOTH TIGERS

STEALTHOR'S FREEZE BLASTA

Stealthor uses a fang-enhanced blaster on missions to scout out the enemy. Powered by CHI, the blaster instantly incapacitates any approaching threat.

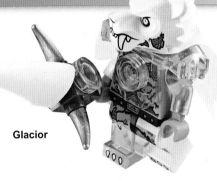

Glacior

Freeze Blasta

SIR FANGAR'S SACRED SWORD

Sir Fanga's triple-pronged sword has been passed down from leader to leader. More decorative than useful, the sword hasn't been used in battle for thousands of years.

MAMMOTHS

Tuskstaff

SHARP STAFFS

These ancient staffs are sacred to the Hunters. The double-headed Tuskstaff is a common weapon for Mammoths, and the Saber-tooth Tigers' clawed Koldstaf is useful for hand-to-hand fighting.

Koldstaf

MAULA'S MAMZOOKA

Maula's Pulsor has a massive caliber. Its huge barrel can blast out a powerful beam of ice, stopping even the biggest of warriors in their tracks.

Mamzooka

VULTURES

EASY DOES IT

Vulture weapons aren't that advanced, mostly because the lazy Vultures can't be bothered to create better ones. Their weapons tend to be simple claw-shaped spears and Pulsorz.

Bonezythe

Chokize

MINIFIGURE GALLERY
2013–2014

Have you spotted Lavertus in his ShadoWind disguise, or found all the heroes of Chima in their new Fire outfits? Look out for Firox—DK's exclusive minifigure, created just for this book!

LAVAL
(Gold armor)

LAVAL
(Silver armor)

LAVAL
(Outlands armor)

LAVAL
(Fire suit)

LAGRAVIS

LAGRAVIS
(Fire suit)

LEONIDAS

LONGTOOTH

LENNOX
(Gold armor)

LENNOX
(Silver armor)

LAVERTUS
(Gold armor)

LAVERTUS
(Silver armor)

LAVERTUS
(ShadoWind
disguise)

CRAGGER
(Gold armor)

CRAGGER
(Silver armor)

CRAGGER
(Outlands armor)

CRAGGER
(Fire suit)

CROMINUS

CROOLER

CRAWLEY

CRUG

ERIS
(Gold armor)

ERIS
(Heavy gold armor)

ERIS
(Outlands armor)

ERIS
(Fire suit)

EQUILA

EGLOR

EWAR

EWALD

RAZAR
(Silver armor)

RAZAR
(Gold armor)

RAZAR
(Fire suit)

RAZCAL
(Silver armor)

RAZCAL
(Heavy silver armor)

RAWZOM

RIZZO

WORRIZ
(Silver armor)

WORRIZ
(Outlands armor)

WORRIZ
(Fire suit)

WINZAR

WILHURT

WINDRA

WAKZ

GORZAN
(Brown armor)

GORZAN
(Outlands armor)

GORZAN
(Silver armor)

GORZAN
(Fire suit)

G'LOONA

GRUMLO

GRIZZAM

ROGON

RINONA

FURTY

SKINNET

BRAPTOR

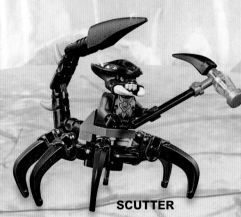

BLISTA

SCORM

SCOLDER

SCUTTER

SPINLYN

SPARACON

SPARRATUS

FLUMINOX

FLUMINOX
(Speedor outfit)

FLINX

FIROX

FRAX

FOLTRAX

TORMAK

LUNDOR

LI'ELLA

SIR FANGAR

STEALTHOR

STRAINOR

SYKOR

MAULA

MUNGUS

MOTTROT

VARDY

VORNON

VOOM VOOM

SET GALLERY

2013–2014

These are all the LEGO® Legends of Chima™ sets released so far. Have you collected the latest ones and joined the battle of Fire Tribes vs. Hunter Tribes?

70000
Razcal's Glider

70001
Crawley's Claw Ripper

70002
Lennox' Lion Attack

70003
Eris' Eagle Interceptor

70004
Wakz' Pack Tracker

70005
Laval's Royal Fighter

70006
Cragger's Command Ship

70007
Eglor's Twin Bike

70008
Gorzan's Gorilla Striker

70009
Worriz's Combat Lair

70010
The Lion CHI Temple

70011
Eagles' Castle

70012
Razar's CHI Raider

70013
Equila's Ultra Striker

70014
The Croc Swamp Hideout

70100
Ring of Fire

70101
Target Practice

70102
CHI Waterfall

70103
Boulder Bowling

70104
Jungle Gates

70105
Nest Dive

70106
Ice Tower

70107
Skunk Attack

70108
Royal Roost

70109
Whirling Vines

70110
Tower Target

70111
Swamp Jump

70112
Croc Chomp

70113
CHI Battles

70114
Sky Joust

70115 Ultimate
Speedor Tournament

70200
CHI Laval

70201
CHI Eris

70202
CHI Gorzan

70203
CHI Cragger

70204
CHI Worriz

70205
CHI Razar

70123 Lion
Legend Beast

70124 Eagle
Legend Beast

70125 Gorilla
Legend Beast

70126 Crocodile
Legend Beast

70127 Wolf
Legend Beast

70128 Braptor's
Wing Striker

70129 Lavertus'
Twin Blade

70130 Sparratus'
Spider Stalker

70131 Rogon's Rock Flinger

70132 Scorm's
Scorpion Stinger

70133 Spinlyn's Cavern

70134 Lavertus' Outland Base

70136
Banana Bash

70137
Bat Strike

70138
Web Dash

70139
Sky Launch

70140
Stinger Duel

70135
Cragger's Fire Striker

70141
Vardy's Ice
Vulture Glider

70142 Eris'
Fire Eagle Flyer

70143 Sir Fangar's
Saber-tooth Walker

70144
Laval's Fire Lion

70145 Maula's Ice
Mammoth Stomper

70146
Flying Phoenix Fire Temple

70147
Sir Fangar's Ice Fortress

70149
Scorching Blades

70150
Flaming Claws

70151
Frozen Spikes

70206
CHI Laval

70207
CHI Cragger

70208
CHI Panthar

70209
CHI Mungus

70155
Inferno Pit

70156
Fire vs. Ice

70210
CHI Vardy

70211
CHI Fluminox

70212
CHI Sir Fangar

LONDON, NEW YORK, MUNICH,
MELBOURNE, AND DELHI

Editor Emma Grange
Designer Richard Horsford
Pre-Production Producer Marc Staples
Senior Producer Lloyd Robertson
Managing Editor Elizabeth Dowsett
Design Manager Ron Stobbart
Art Director Lisa Lanzarini
Publishing Manager Julie Ferris
Publishing Director Simon Beecroft

Designed for DK by Dynamo Ltd.

First published in the United States in 2014
by DK Publishing
345 Hudson Street, New York,
New York 10014

10 9 8 7 6 5 4 3 2 1
001—198547—Aug/14

Page design © 2014 Dorling Kindersley

Discover more at
www.dk.com
www.LEGO.com

ACKNOWLEDGMENTS
Dorling Kindersley would like to thank
Randi Sørensen, Robert Stefan Ekblom,
Samuel Thomas Johnson, Andrew
Woodman, Tommy Andreasen,
Craig Callum, Phil McCormick, Tim Ainley,
Alexandre Boudon, Christian Damm, Daire
McCabe, Hans Burkhard Schlömer, Mark
Stafford, Adrian Florea, Martin Klotz, Luka
Kapeter, Junya Suzuki, Søren Gehlert Dyrhøj,
Callan Kemp, Michael Svane Knap, Gabriel Sas,
Andre Sang-Tae Stenbryggen, Tore Magelund
Harmark-Alexandersen, Flavia Ivanoff, Kurt
Meysmans, Kjeld Walther Sørensen, Christoffer
Raundahl, and Esben Fløe at the LEGO Group;
Ruth Amos, Jo Casey, and Beth Davies
for their editorial work; Anne Sharples and
Elena Jarmoskaite for design work, and Gary
Ombler for his extra photography.

DK books are available at special discounts when purchased in bulk
for sales promotions, premiums, fund-raising, or educational use.
For details, contact: DK Publishing, Special Markets, 4th Floor,
345 Hudson Street, New York, New York 10014
SpecialSales@dk.com

A catalog record for this book is available from the Library of Congress.

ISBN: 978-1-4654-1666-7

Color reproduction
in the UK by Altaimage.
Printed and bound in China
by Leo Paper Products Ltd.